CORRUPTION AND NIGERIAN FOREIGN POLICY (1999 – 2007)

BY

UDDOH, JUDE CHIGBO
(G2007/PHD/POL/FT/353)

DEPARTMENT OF POLITICAL AND ADMINISTRATIVE STUDIES
FACULTY OF SOCIAL SCIENCES

BEING

A DOCTOR OF PHILOSOPHY DISSERTATION

SUBMITTED TO

THE SCHOOL OF GRADUATE STUDIES
UNIVERSITY OF PORT HARCOURT

SUPERVISOR:

DR. GEORGE OBUOFORIBO

FEBRUARY 2012

CORRUPTION AND NIGERIAN FOREIGN POLICY (1999 - 2007)

JUDE UDDOH, PH.D.

authorHOUSE®

AuthorHouse™
1663 Liberty Drive
Bloomington, IN 47403
www.authorhouse.com
Phone: 1 (800) 839-8640

Published by AuthorHouse 01/15/2016

ISBN: 978-1-5049-7404-2 (sc)
ISBN: 978-1-5049-7405-9 (e)

Print information available on the last page.

This book is printed on acid-free paper.

CONTENTS

CERTIFICATION

This is to certify that this dissertation is the original work of the candidate Uddoh, Jude Chigbo and that it has been read and approved as meeting the requirements for the award of a Doctor of Philosophy (Ph.D.) degree from the Department of Political and Administrative Studies, Faculty of Social Science, University of Port Harcourt, Rivers State, Nigeria.

_____   _____
DR. GEORGE OBUOFORIBO   DATE
(SUPERVISOR)

_____   _____
DR. EME EKEKWE   DATE
(HEAD OF DEPARTMENT)

_____   _____
PROFESSOR HENRY ALAPIKI   DATE
(DEAN, FACULTY OF SOCIAL SCIENCE)

_____   _____
PROFESSOR SAM C. EGWU   DATE
(EXTERNAL EXAMINER)

DEDICATION

To the memory of my late parents –
Patrick Nzeama Uddoh and Catherine Ezeagbo Uddoh

ACKNOWLEDGEMENT

I thank God Almighty through whose divine providence this work is made possible. I am grateful to the Dean of the School of Graduate Studies; Dean, Faculty of Social Sciences – Prof. Henry Alapiki; Head of the Department of Political and Administrative Studies – Dr. Eme Ekekwe, and all the lecturers in the International Relations unit particularly my past and present supervisors Professor O. J. B. Ojo and Dr. George Obuoforibo. I am also very thankful to the external examiner - Professor Sam Egwu, for his profound contribution to this work.

I acknowledge the support I received from various organizations in the course of this work in particular, the Center for Advanced Social Studies (CASS) Port Harcourt; Zero Corruption Tolerance Lagos; Transparency International Berlin; Nigerian Institute of International Affairs (NIIA) Lagos; Nigerian Investment Promotion Commission (NIPC) Abuja; Dr. Cyril U. Gwam of the Ministry of Foreign Affairs (MOFA) Abuja, and the University of Columbia Libraries, NY.

I am grateful for the support of my family members particularly Dr. Christopher Uddoh; Engr. Maurice Uddoh; Chief Mike Udo; Dr. I. U. Mbeledeogu; and Mr. Moses Udoh. I am also grateful for the companionship of all my colleagues at the Graduate Hall of Residence University of Port Harcourt, particularly, Dr. Jude Ikporukpo and Mr. Chris Olele. Finally, my gratitude goes to my wife Cynthia, and our children Esther, Patrick, and Junior for bearing with me through this long and tedious academic task.

I most humbly accept responsibility for all errors and mistakes in this work.

Jude Chigbo Uddoh
February 2012

ABSTRACT

Nigeria's foreign policy has always been predicated on the national interest which is reducible to the security and welfare of its citizens. Nigeria's position in Africa, its teeming population and rich endowment of mineral resources including oil, all contributed to the notion of Nigeria's manifest leadership in Africa and beyond. Through what became known as an Afro-centrist foreign policy, Nigeria championed the cause of liberating Africa from apartheid and colonial rule. Nigeria sent troops to peace missions in various conflict zones in Africa and other parts of the world, and contributed financially and materially to the well-being of fellow African as well as Caribbean states. Nigeria thus earned for itself the image of a responsible and well-respected member of the international community.

National interest is the thread that runs through both domestic and foreign policies, but corruption is the antithesis of national interest. Corruption is the single most critical factor attributable to Nigeria's political instability and economic stagnation. Corruption explains the Nigerian paradox of poverty in the midst of plenty. A deadly concoction was brewed when the prolonged period of military rule in Nigeria accompanied by disrespect for the rule of law and abuse of human rights, mixed with the perception of Nigeria as one of the most corrupt countries in global terms. Nigeria's hard-earned image was poisoned, and the country plummeted from its renown as the "Giant of Africa" to "a rogue state" and "a nation of scammers." The international community imposed sanctions against Nigeria, and relegated the country to pariah status.

The central problem of our work is to study the dialectic of how corruption has impacted on Nigeria's foreign policy on the one hand, and how Nigeria has fought corruption at the respective domestic, regional and global levels on the other hand. Rosenau's linkage theory provides us with a framework for understanding that the international environment reacts to actions emanating from national polities. The linkage theory is perhaps, the social science equivalent of Newton's third law of motion, which states that "for every action, there is an equal and opposite reaction."

The qualitative rather than quantitative paradigm is adopted for this research, because corruption as a phenomenon is secretive and not open to observation. Hence, participants are unlikely to divulge self-incriminating information. Our approach is therefore historical, descriptive and analytical.

We find that corruption impedes Nigerian foreign policy through loss of image which is the psychological component of its national power, lack of foreign direct investment (FDI)/divestment, depletion of external reserves/accumulation of foreign debts, and harassment of Nigerian citizens abroad. Nigeria has fought corruption albeit with mixed results, at the respective domestic level through the establishment of two anti-corruption agencies (ACAs) – the ICPC and EFCC. At the regional level, Nigeria became a state party to the respective ECOWAS Protocol on the Fight against Corruption, as well as the AU Convention on Preventing and Combating Corruption. At the global level, Nigeria also signed and ratified the United Nations Convention against Corruption (UNCAC).

This study suggests that in order for Nigeria to achieve its foreign policy objectives, the country must first get its domestic priorities right. We advocate an admixture of legal and diplomatic solutions aimed towards strengthening Nigeria's fight against corruption at both unilateral and multilateral levels, as well as improving on the country's battered international image.

Chapter One

1.1 Introduction and Background to Study:

The objectives of Nigerian foreign policy as enunciated by the country's first Prime Minister - Alhaji (Sir) Abubakar Tafawa Balewa, are predicated on the national interest of the federation and its citizens (see also Section 19 [a] of the Constitution of the Federal Republic of Nigeria, 1999). The multi-ethnic nature of Nigeria with over 250 ethnic groups, its in-built cleavages and dysfunctional inequities has made the definition of national interest and consensus building on major issues very problematic (Mustapha: 2008). However, the role and significance of the national interest in relation to the country's foreign policy cannot be overemphasized;

> National interest is a holy grail, not only because it clarifies the foreign policy choices, but also because it sets the rule of engagement within the context of clashing and competing interests in the global arena. It serves as the red lines in the sand against which a country can measure the success of every foreign policy activity (Uhomoibhi: 2011).

The official definition of Nigeria's national interest is contained in the Second National Development Plan, 1970-74, as follows:

- A united, strong and self-reliant nation;
- A great and dynamic economy;
- A just and egalitarian society;
- A land of bright and full opportunities for all citizens; and
- A free and democratic society

National interest is the thread that runs through both domestic and foreign policies. It represents "the aggregation of the principal demands

1

of citizens for such core values as economic and social welfare, national security, social justice and good government" (Akindele: 1990).

Sir Tafawa Balewa made Africa the cornerstone of Nigerian foreign policy. The so-called Balewa doctrine is predicated on Nigeria's location in Africa, its teeming population and rich endowment of mineral resources including oil, all of which contributed to the notion of Nigeria's manifest leadership destiny in Africa and beyond. This perception crystallized to what became known as Nigeria's "Afro-centric" policy after the Nigerian civil war (1967 – 1970), with five broad strands – support for the OAU (now AU); anti-colonial preoccupation; identification with anti-apartheid front; promotion of intra-African cooperation; and commitment to peaceful settlement of inter-state disputes and conflicts (Olusanya and Akindele: 1986).

As a founding member of the Organization of African Unity (OAU), now African Union (AU), Nigeria conducted its "big brother" policy towards the rest of Africa through the OAU, or in line with its principles. Thus, Nigeria played significant roles in the OAU's decision to recognize the Movimento Popular de Libertação de Angola (MPLA). Nigeria also played a part in the independence of Zimbabwe in the late 1980s, as well as making financial contributions to the South West Africa People's Organization (SWAPO) for Namibia's independence. Nigeria further made financial and other material contributions to the African National Congress (ANC) in South Africa, and to the frontline states of Zambia, Tanzania, and Mozambique (Metz: 1991)

Nigeria's role in the liberation of the African continent from colonial rule and apartheid, its participation in peacekeeping missions across Africa and beyond, as well as various other goodwill gestures including the Technical Aid Corp (TAC), assistance through the African Development Bank (ADB) and sale of oil at concessionary rates to African states to mention a few, kept the country's international image and reputation in good standing over the years.

Corruption is the antithesis of national interest. Defined by The World Bank (1997) as, "the abuse of public power for private gain," corruption in Nigeria has been traced to the colonial public service between 1945 and 1960, and has pervaded virtually every administration in the history of Nigeria whether military or civilian since independence.

Corruption in the Nigerian colonial public service took mainly three forms – bribery or the giving of money or goods to obtain favour, facilitate service, or influence the judgment of someone in a position of authority; misappropriation, usually of public funds for private ends; and nepotism or the bestowing of patronage on the basis of ethnic or sub-ethnic identities (Falola: 1998).

There are conflicting accounts of precisely when corruption reached its peak in Nigeria. In his testimony before the US Congress, Nuhu Ribadu – the former Chairman of the Economic and Financial Crimes Commission (EFCC) termed the period between 1979 and 1998 "the darkest period" in Nigeria's history of corrupt regimes. According to him, the Shagari administration (1979 – 1983) was bedeviled with profligacy, wanton waste, political thuggery and coercion, disrespect for the rule of law, bare faced and free for all looting of public funds through white elephant projects;

> Corrupt public servants and others in the private sector bestrode the nation, masquerading as captains of business and power brokers with tainted and stolen wealth (Ribadu: 2006).

Another account has it that corruption became legitimized in Nigeria during the respective regimes of General Ibrahim Babangida (1985 – 1993) and General Sani Abacha (1993 - 1998), both of which were characterized by huge revenues but wasteful spending, and nothing to show in terms of physical development.

Whatever be the case, it is on record that Transparency International through its annual Corruption Perception Index (CPI) ranked Nigeria as the most corrupt country in global terms in 1996 and 1997 consecutively during the Abacha regime, and again in 2000 during the Obasanjo administration. Nigeria's cumulative average position in the CPI from 1996 to 2007 – a period of twelve years is 2.83, hardly an enviable position by any standard. Without any doubt, corruption in Nigeria moved from a matter of perception to a serious cultural problem;

The culture of corruption through what Nigerians have come to know as settlement syndrome became part of the country's political culture. All the positive values for development were jettisoned. Government agencies that were the pilot of socioeconomic development were decimated (Sowunmi et al: 2010).

In response to the Abacha regime's execution of Ken Saro-Wiwa and 8 other Ogoni activists in November 1995, the Commonwealth suspended Nigeria's membership. The United Nations also indicted the regime for its poor human rights record. Several other countries including South Africa recalled their ambassadors and imposed limited sanctions against Nigeria including visa restrictions on military personnel and government officials, suspension of military cooperation, and boycott of sporting contacts.

A combination of endemic corruption in Nigeria, and prolonged military rule with its attendant human rights abuse and disregard for the rule of law, transformed Nigeria from a once respected member of the international community into a "rogue" state. The purpose of our research is to investigate into the impact of corruption on Nigerian foreign policy, and how Nigeria has responded to the problem of corruption at the domestic level, as well as its collaboration with other countries and the international community at the respective regional and global levels in the anti-corruption realm.

1.2 Statement of the Research Problem

Corruption constitutes perhaps the single most critical domestic challenge to Nigeria's political stability, economic development and social cohesion. According to Obasanjo (2000);

Corruption has been responsible for the instability of successive governments since the First Republic. Every coup since then has been in the name of stamping out the disease called corruption. Unfortunately, the cure often turned out to be worse than the disease. And

Nigeria has been the worse for it. Nigeria's external image took a serious bashing, as our beloved country began to feature on top of every corruption index.

The former President of the World Bank – Paul Wolfowitz estimates that Nigeria lost over $300 billion to corruption between 1970 and 2001, a feature which has held back economic growth and development and frustrated incentives to align budgetary allocations with development priorities. Corruption accounts for the Nigerian paradox of poverty in the midst of plenty; In spite of being the eighth largest producer of oil in the world, Nigeria has the world's third largest poor people, with about 75% of the people living on less than a dollar per day (APRM: 2008).

The constraints that corruption poses to Nigeria's domestic polity also extend to its foreign policy. Nuamah (2003) notes the connection as follows;

> Corruption in Nigeria constrains the country's economic development and consequently its economic and political reach regionally and internationally.

During Nigeria's First Republic under Alhaji (Sir) Abubakar Tafawa Balewa, Nnamdi Azikiwe was indicted for abusing his office by allowing public funds to be invested in African Continental Bank (ACB) in which he had interests. Chief Obafemi Awolowo was also found guilty of diverting N4.4 million in cash and N1.3 million in overdraft from the Western Region Government-owned National Investment and Property Company, to finance the Action Group (AG) party and to build a personal financial empire (Osaghae: 1998). Izah (1991) contends that the internal problems of "regionalism, tribalism, nepotism and corruption" account for much of the economic and political weakness of the First Republic, robbing it of a strong and virile foreign policy and eventually leading to its downfall.

The regime of General Ibrahim Babangida is particularly remembered for blowing $12.4 billion Gulf war oil windfall accruing to Nigeria through the so-called "dedicated and special" accounts, in extra-budgetary expenditures over a period of about six years (Oko-Osi: 2007).

Transparency International estimates that General Sani Abacha and his associates stole between $2 billion and $5 billion from the Nigerian treasury, and ranked him among the top five political looters of all time. Between May 1995 and February 1998 in what the former Chairman of the Economic and Financial Crimes Commission (EFCC) Nuhu Ribadu described as the single biggest advanced fee fraud case in the whole world, four Nigerian nationals Christian Anajemba, Emmanuel Nwude, Nzeribe Okoli and Amaka Anajemba defrauded Banco Noroeste S.A. of Brazil of a total of $242 million on the pretext of securing contracts for the construction of a second international airport in Abuja, the Federal Capital Territory (FCT).

Cumulatively, the period that began in 1985 is described as constituting an interesting watershed for the present and future of Nigerian foreign policy. A hostile external environment intensively dominated by the worldwide economic recession of the 1980s, the consequent adverse effects on Nigeria's foreign exchange earnings, rampant internal corruption, and excessive personalization of decision making combined to weaken the thrust and effectiveness of Nigerian foreign policy. These circumstances caused Nigerian foreign policy to weaken and lose scope (Abegunrin: 2003).

Some cases of grand corruption during the Third Republic administration of President Olusegun Obasanjo that captured the attention of both domestic and international audience include conviction of Inspector General of Police Tafa Balogun on an 8-count charge of money laundering and forfeiture of assets totaling $150 million; conviction of Governor Diepreye Alamieyesegha of Bayelsa State on a 6-count charge of false declaration of assets and a 23-count charge by his companies of money laundering, leading to recovery of over $17.7 million in stolen assets; conviction of Deputy National Chairman PDP and Chairman Nigerian Ports Authority – Chief Olabode George and five others on a 35-count charge of contract inflation by about N100 billion among others; and conviction of Delta State Governor James Ibori by a London court on a 10-count charge of conspiracy to defraud and money laundering estimated at $250 million.

Nothing could have been more humiliating for Nigeria as a nation, than the image of its governors, symbols of the country's sovereignty and political leadership, being paraded in foreign courts on corruption-related charges. After fifty years of political independence, Jega (2010) reached the verdict that weak economic and political structures, ineffective institutions and processes, and bad governance, characterized by quarrelsome, inept and corrupt public officers, have combined to undermine the influence and respectability that ought to have accrued to Nigeria's foreign policy undertakings.

The image of a responsible and well respected member of the international community which Nigeria cut for itself since independence through its active role in the liberation of African countries from colonial rule, as well as its contributions to peacekeeping in Africa and beyond among others, was completed eroded and replaced by the image of a rogue state - a nation of scammers, when beginning from 1996, Transparency International ranked Nigeria as one of the most corrupt countries in global terms in its annual Corruption Perception Index (CPI) thus, substantially distorting the image and goodwill of the country.

The high incidence of corruption in Nigeria including the practice of advance fee fraud (AFF) has not only contributed to damaging Nigeria's image abroad, but has also made it more difficult for the country to attract the much needed foreign direct investment (FDI) as several countries and jurisdictions including the Bureau of Consular Affairs of the U.S. Department of State; the British Foreign and Commonwealth Office; and the Canadian Department of Foreign Affairs and International Trade have issued travel and communication advisories restricting business interactions between their citizens and Nigeria (UNCTAD: 2009).

Divestment from Nigeria became the order of the day. Over 150 multinational corporations (MNCs) divested from Nigeria since 1985, while more than 60 per cent of local industries, mostly small scale enterprises folded up since 1986, when the Babangida regime introduced the Structural Adjustment Programme. MNCs that reduced their holdings in Nigeria during the Abacha regime include Standard Chartered Bank, the Wellcome Foundation, and Unilever Plc. The exodus of MNCs from Nigeria during the Obasanjo administration includes Michelin, Dunlop, Pfizer, Aventis, GlaxoWellcome and

SmithKline Beecham (GlaxoSmithKline), Hoescht and Procter and Gamble (P&G) (Osaghae: 1998).

The impact of Nigeria's global image and reputation for corruption was not lost on Nigerians living or travelling abroad, as many of them were subjected to unnecessary harassment by such foreign agencies as immigration, customs and the police. In many instances, Nigerians were singled out from queues at international airports and kept waiting for hours or subjected to humiliating bodily searches. Even members of the Nigerian diplomatic corp were not spared the humiliation, but were also subjected to the same kind of treatment, clearly in breach of their diplomatic immunity and privileges. Hence, the Nigerian Government has had cause to lodge formal protests with the European Union (EU), the United Nations (UN) and other international organizations on account of the ill-treatment being meted out to its citizens overseas based sometimes on unwarranted suspicion.

Without doubt, corruption poses severe and profound challenges to Nigerian foreign policy. Therefore, the pertinent questions that we intend to address in this research include the following:

- What are the historical antecedents of the interaction between corruption and Nigerian foreign policy?
- What are the broad typologies of corruption during the administration of President Olusegun Obasanjo?
- What is the impact of corruption on Nigerian foreign policy?
- How has Nigeria responded to the challenges posed by corruption at the domestic, regional and global levels respectively?
- How can Nigeria minimize the damage of corruption on its international image and foreign policy?

1.3   Objectives of the Study

The objectives of our study may be summarized as follows:

(a) To examine the historical antecedents of the interaction between corruption and Nigerian foreign policy.

(b) To highlight the broad typologies of corruption during the Obasanjo administration.

(c) To identify the impact of corruption on Nigerian foreign policy.

(d) To examine Nigeria's response to the challenge of corruption at the respective domestic, regional and global levels.

(e) To proffer some suggestions on how Nigeria could consolidate and advance on progress made in its anti-corruption drive.

1.4 Research Statements

Our study will be guided by the following research statements:

- The conduct of a country's foreign policy is to complement domestic imperatives of maximizing the welfare and security of citizens;

- Nigeria's endemic culture of corruption has undermined domestic desires for achieving the purpose of the state and particularly, has negatively impacted on the country's international image and foreign policy; and

- Responding to Nigeria's corruption at home and abroad has played a critical role in shaping Nigerian foreign policy under the Obasanjo administration.

1.5 Theoretical Framework

For the purpose of this study, we shall adopt as our theoretical framework James N. Rosenau's linkage theory (Rosenau: 1969). The purpose of linkage theory as propounded by Rosenau is to identify points at which national systems and international systems overlap and to precipitate thought about the nature and scope of the phenomena that fall within the area of overlap.

The Concept of a Linkage

Rosenau defines linkage as "any recurrent sequence of behavior that originates in one system and is reacted to in another." Polity stands for the national political system, while environment refers to the international system which is external to the polity. Polity outputs originate from the polity and terminate in the environment as inputs, while environmental outputs originate from the environment and terminate in the polity as inputs (Figure 1.1).

Figure 1.1 Rosenau's Stages of Linkage

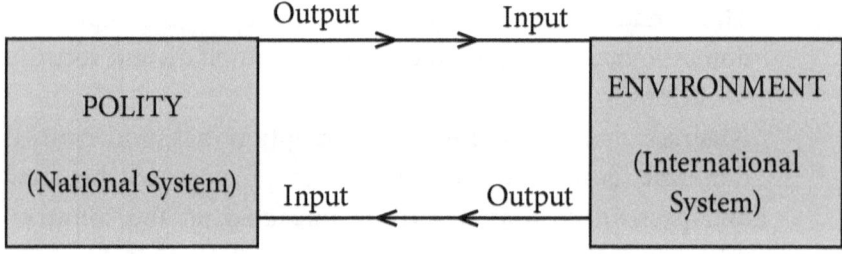

Adapted from Rosenau (1969)

Note that the boundaries between national and international systems can be crossed by processes of perception and emulation, as well as by direct interaction. Note also that some outputs evoke direct response from another system. These are called direct outputs. Other patterns of behavior are not meant to evoke boundary-crossing responses, but nevertheless do so through perception or emulative processes. These are called indirect outputs.

The difference between the case method and the linkage theory is that whereas single occurrences could form the basis of analysis in the former, in the latter, there must be multiple or recurrent sequences of events (outputs/inputs). A further distinctive category of the linkage theory is the fused linkage, in which sequences of outputs and inputs form a reciprocal relationship in such a way that they cannot be meaningfully analyzed separately.

The Components of a Linkage Framework

Rosenau develops the linkage theory by expanding the output/input sequence into a larger framework comprising 24 sub-categories of the polity, broadly outlined under 5 headings, namely, actors, attitudes, institutions, and processes on the one hand, and 6 sub-categories of the environment, namely, the contiguous environment, the regional environment, the Cold War environment, the racial environment, the resource environment, and the organizational environment on the other hand.

Table 1.2 Rosenau's Linkage Theory Matrix

Environment ⟶ (Outputs/Inputs) Polity ↓	The Contiguous Env.	The Regional Env.	The Cold War Env.	The Racial Env.	The Resource Env.	The Organizational Env.
Actors:						
1. Executive Officials						
2. Legislative Officials						
3. Civilian Bureaucracies						
1. Military Bureaucracies						
2. Political parties						
3. Interest Groups						
4. Elite Group						
Attitudes:						
5. Ideology						
6. Political Culture						
7. Public Opinion						
Institutions:						
8. Executive						
9. Legislatures						
10. Bureaucracies						
11. Military Establishment						
12. Elections						
13. Party Systems						

14. Communication Systems						
15. Social Institutions						
Processes: 16. Socialization/ Recruitment						
17. Interest Articulation						
18. Interest Aggregation						
19. Policy Making						
20. Policy Administration						
21. Integrative/ Disintegrative						

Source: Rosenau (1969)

The resulting matrix of 24 actor sub-categories × 6 environment sub-categories, yields 144 areas in which national-international linkages can be formed (Table 1.2).

<u>Relating the Linkage Theory to the Present Study</u>

Rosenau's linkage theory helps us to analyze corruption and its impacts as recurrent sequences of behavior that originates from the Nigerian polity and is reacted to in the international environment. Corruption emanating from the Nigerian polity is termed "policy output," which either culminates or is sustained by the international system as "environmental input." Similarly, "environmental output" are those sequences of behavior that start in the external environment in reaction to corruption, which either terminates in or is sustained within the Nigerian polity as "polity input."

In order to fit into theory building, both corruption as a polity output and the corresponding environmental output which it generates from the international system, must recur with sufficient frequency to form a pattern. In other words, they must not be conceived to be a single event or occurrence as with the case method.

Corruption in the Nigerian polity and international reaction to it is neither restricted to a single occurrence nor to any single administration.

As our undertaking of a historical perspective of the interaction between corruption and Nigerian foreign policy in Chapter Three indicates, the phenomenon of corruption in the Nigerian polity has been traced to the colonial public service between 1945 and 1960, and has pervaded virtually every administration both civilian and military in the post-independence era (Falola: 1998). Similarly, the international system has consistently reacted to corruption in Nigeria through such measures as restrictions in foreign direct investment/divestment from the country and isolation/relegation of Nigeria to pariah status, among others.

The linkage matrix provides a template for analyzing the resultant interaction between corruption and foreign policy based on multiple categories of the Nigerian polity (executive, legislative, military, bureaucracy, political parties, elections, etc.) and the reaction to it from different categories of the environment or international system such as the formation of multilateral anticorruption conventions at the respective regional (ECOWAS Protocol on the Fight against Corruption/ AU Convention on Preventing and Combating Corruption) and global (United Nations Convention against Corruption) levels.

As noted above, the boundaries between national and international systems can be crossed by processes of perception and emulation, as well as by direct interaction. The Corruption Perception Index (CPI) published annually by Transparency International is a perfect example of how corruption crosses the boundary between the Nigerian polity and the international environment by a process of perception. The CPI ranks countries according to the level that respondents perceive corruption to exist among their politicians and public officials. Even though this subjective perception may not reflect the objective reality, yet the CPI has become a powerful tool for ranking the level of corruption on a cross-border basis and constitutes the chief instrument for the consistent finding of Nigeria as one of the most corrupt countries in global terms.

The image that Nigeria projects through its foreign policy as well as its perception by the domestic and external audience form part of a complex relationship referred to as the concept of national image. National image dwells in the psychological realm, but is nevertheless a vital component of national power along with other more tangible components such as industrial or military capability (Ogwu: 2005).

While Nigeria has consistently projected a "leadership" image through its Afro-centrist foreign policy, the country has been more apt, especially in recent times, to be perceived as "a nation of scammers' because of its global image and reputation for corruption thus further underscoring Rosenau's linkage theory (Jega: 2010).

On the other hand, direct linkage between the national polity and international system is demonstrated by 'Grand' or 'Political' corruption in developing countries, which is financed by foreign trade and investors and goes to politicians and senior officials (Short: 1999). Typically, foreign multinational corporations (MNCs) from the industrial nations bribe politicians and public officials from the developing countries to obtain lucrative contracts. A number of these cases are discussed in Chapter Four of the study, but an example will suffice here. The Shagari administration entered a contract with British Aerospace for the supply of eighteen Jaguar jets at an inflated rate of £300 million, from which NPN stalwarts were alleged to have received 'kickbacks' of £22 million (Osaghae: 1998).

Often, as we have seen in the case of General Sani Abacha, Governor Diepreye Alamieyesegha, and Governor James Ibori etc., it is in foreign bank accounts that the corrupt Nigerian public officials stash their ill-gotten wealth, thus providing another direct and critical part of the corruption linkage between the Nigerian polity and its international environment. Hence, asset recovery has become an indispensable part of most international anti-corruption conventions.

The vicious circle in which MNCs from industrialized nations collaborate with politicians and public officials in developing countries to perpetrate political/grand corruption and the stashing of the ill-gotten wealth in foreign bank accounts constitute what Roseanu describes as a "fused" linkage, whereby sequences of outputs and inputs form a reciprocal and inseparable relationship. The Economist captures what practically constitutes a double jeopardy for Africa in its relations with Europe as a result of corruption in the following terms;

> Official corruption siphons off money intended for
> Africa. Apart from making a lot of profit on the interest
> on investment accruing from Africa's stolen money,

Europeans turn around and loan such money to Africa at exorbitant rates.

Other examples of the fused linkage between the Nigerian polity and the international environment in the corruption discourse, exists in the form of multilateral anti-corruption conventions discussed in Chapter Five, whereby several countries are linked at the national, regional or global levels in their mutual desire to provide a common front to fight what has been recognized as a cross-border phenomenon. Exploring the linkage between corruption and foreign policy, Liken (1996) observes that corruption has become the subject matter of international treaties and assistance programs, and has preoccupied international economic organizations as well as intelligence and law enforcement agencies.

Disadvantages of the Linkage Theory

One of the major disadvantages of the linkage theory is that the various categories of national polities and their international environments are imprecise, incomplete, impressionistic, and overlapping. As Roseau himself admits, "further refinement would no doubt result in the merging of some categories and the replacement of others."

Rosenau defines foreign policy in the context of national-international linkages, as;

> Recurring forms of action or inaction that the duly constituted authorities of a polity initiate towards one or more objects in their external environment, with a view to either preventing the object from hindering the satisfaction of polity needs and wants or obtaining resources from it that will facilitate satisfaction of polity needs (Rosenau; 1969: 54).

He also recognizes the impact that non-governmental organizations e.g. multinational corporations (MNCs) and distinguished citizens make, with the intention of preserving or altering one or more aspects of the polity's external environment. However, non-conformist behavior by private citizens, such as the involvement of private Nigerian citizens in advance fee fraud (AFF) which nevertheless impacts on the international environment albeit negatively, is not contemplated within the framework of the linkage matrix. This is akin to the definition of corruption as "the abuse of public power for private gain (The World Bank: 1997), which also does not make ample provision for private sector corruption such as AFF.

Advantages of the Linkage Theory

Rosenau's linkage theory compels thought about the way in which comparative and international politics are linked. Corruption regained prominence in international discourse since the 1990s as "a truly global political issue eliciting a global political response (Glynn et al: 1997). At the same time, the cross border research of organizations like Transparency International, serve to highlight differences between national as well as regional corruption traits, hence developing countries are generally perceived to be more corrupt than industrialized nations.

But the most important advantage of the linkage theory perhaps, is that it provides the social science equivalent of Newton's third law of motion which states that for every action there is an equal and opposite reaction, in the sense that there are international reactions to corruption emanating from the Nigerian polity. As our research shows, corruption in Nigeria elicits negative reactions from the international environment including loss of image, international isolation, lack of foreign direct investment (FDI) and divestment, depletion of external reserves and accumulation of foreign debts, and harassment of Nigerian citizens abroad.

1.6 Scope of Study

The scope of our study focuses on the subjects of corruption and Nigerian foreign policy within the timeframe of President Olusegun Obasanjo's administration (1999 – 2007). The period witnessed momentous events and developments in the key variables under study. They include Transparency International's ranking of Nigeria as the most corrupt country in its 2000 Corruption Perception Index (CPI), under a democratically elected civilian government. Nigeria also undertook very ambitious anti-corruption policy measures within this period including the establishment of two domestic anti-corruption institutions – the Independent Corrupt Practices and other Related Offences Commission (ICPC) and the Economic and Financial Crimes Commission (EFCC), as well as signing up to several multilateral anti-corruption treaties and conventions, including the ECOWAS Protocol on the Fight against Corruption (signed 2001); the AU Convention on Preventing and Combating Corruption (Signed Dec. 16, 2003), and the UN Convention against Corruption (Signed Dec. 9, 2003/ratified Dec. 14, 2004). However, we have also examined the interaction between corruption and Nigerian foreign policy in a historical perspective, in order to gain insight and broaden our understanding of the relationship between the variables under study.

1.7 Significance of Study

Our study significantly identifies and explains how corruption links Nigeria as a national polity with the international environment. In other words, corruption in Nigeria produces a complex web of interaction and relationship between the domestic and external environments of the country's foreign policy. Whereas on the one hand, elements of the international environment in the form of MNCs collaborate with Nigerian politicians and public officials to perpetrate political/grand corruption, we also observe international reaction against corruption in the Nigerian polity, in the form of withdrawal of foreign direct investment (FDI) and divestment from Nigeria etc., on the other hand. Yet on another hand, there is international collaboration between the Nigerian polity and the external environment at the respective regional and global levels in the anti-corruption realm. Multilateral anti-corruption conventions to which Nigeria is a state party include the ECOWAS Protocol on the Fight against Corruption; the AU Convention on Preventing and Combating Corruption; as well as the United Nations Convention against Corruption (UNCAC).

1.8 Approach to the Study

We adopt the qualitative rather than quantitative paradigm for this research due to the nature of the phenomenon under study. Corruption is an activity that usually takes place in secret where it cannot be openly observed, and participants are unlikely to provide information which could be self-incriminating. According to Mcmullan (1970: 318):

> Arguments and statements about corruption cannot be demonstrated by factual or statistical evidence. Corruption is not a subject which can be investigated openly by means of questionnaires and interviews. Even if it were, in principle, possible to quantify the phenomenon, there would be no practical possibility of doing so.

Our method for conducting this study is therefore historical, descriptive and analytical. The descriptive method is defined as the scientific collection of information to describe an existing phenomenon. The method is deductive and involves the processes of identifying the problems, making comparisons, and finally making systematic evaluation (Ofo: 1994). A significant advantage of the descriptive method is that it enables us to discover efforts made by other researchers to solve similar problems and to build on their progress. We rely on several secondary sources of information for this research including standard texts, opinion based surveys, courts indictment and legal proceedings, statistical data from relevant agencies, media sources, and expert opinion.

1.9 Organization of the Study

The study is organized into six chapters. Chapter One outlines introduction and background to the study; statement of the research problem; objectives of the study; research statements; theoretical framework; scope of study; significance of study; Aaproach to the Study; and organization of the study. Chapter Two contains a review of the relevant literature. Chapter Three sets out a historical perspective of corruption and Nigerian foreign policy. Chapter Four deals with corruption and Nigerian foreign policy under President Olusegun Obasanjo's administration. Chapter Five deals with Nigerian foreign policy and the challenge of corruption. Chapter Six contains our conclusion; summary of findings; and suggestions.

References
Chapter One

Abegunrin, Olayiwola (2003) *Nigerian Foreign Policy under Military Rule, 1966-1999* Westport, Praeger Publishers

Akindele, R. A. (1990) "Coordination of Domestic and Foreign Policies: Reflections on Institutional Structure and Political Processes" in Olusanya, Gabriel O. and Akindele, R. A. (Eds) (1990) *The Structure and Processes of Foreign Policy Making and Implementation in Nigeria, 1960 – 1990* Lagos, NIIA Pp. 243 – 251

APRM (2008) *Federal Republic of Nigeria. Country Review Report No. 8.* South Africa, African Peer Review Mechanism

Falola, Toyin (1998) "Corruption in the Nigerian Public Service: 1945 – 1960" in Mbaku, John M. (1998) *Corruption and the Crisis of Institutional Reforms in Africa* Lewinson, Edwin Mellen Press Pp. 137 – 163.

Glynn Patrick, Kobrin Stephen J, Naim Moises (1997) *The Globalization of Corruption* Institute for International Economics http://www.iie.com

Izah, Paul P. (1991) *Continuity and Change in Nigerian Foreign Policy* Zaria, Ahmadu Bello University Press

Jega, Attahiru M. (2010) "Nigeria's Foreign Policy and the Promotion of Peace, Development, and Democracy," in Jega, Attahiru M. and Farris, Jacqueline W. (Eds.) (2010) *Nigeria at Fifty: Contributions to Peace, Democracy and Development* Abuja, The Shehu Musa Yar'Adua Foundation

Leiken, Robert S. (1996) *Controlling the Global Corruption Epidemic* Foreign Policy No. 105 (Winter, 1996-1997) Pp. 55 – 73.

Macmullan, M., (1970) "Corruption in the Public Service of British Colonies and Ex-Colonies in West Africa" in Heidenheimer, Arnold J.,

Ed. (1970) *Political Corruption: Readings in Comparative Analysis* New Jersey, Transaction Books. Pp. 317-330

Metz, Helen C. (Ed) (1991) *Nigeria: A Case Study.* Washington, Library of Congress

Mustapha, Abdul Raufu (2008) "The Three Faces of Nigeria's Foreign Policy: Nationhood, Identity and External Relations" in Adebajo, Adekeye and Mustapha, Abdul Raufu (2008) Gulliver's Trouble: Nigeria's Foreign Policy after the Cold War University of KwaZulu-Natal Press, South Africa pp. 41 – 57.

Nuamah, Rosemary (Rpt) (2003) *Nigeria's Foreign Policy after the Cold War: Domestic, Regional and External Influences* Oxford, University of Oxford.

Ofo, Janet E. (1994) *Research Methods and Statistics in Education and Social Sciences* Lagos, Joja Publishers Ltd.

Olusanya G. O. and Akindele R. A. (1986) "The Fundamentals of Nigeria's Foreign Policy and External economic Relations" in Olusanya G. O. and Akindele R. A. (Eds) (1986) *Nigeria's External Relations: The First Twenty Five Years* Ibadan, The University Press Limited Pp. 1 – 32

Osaghae, Eghosa E. (1998) *Crippled Giant: Nigeria since Independence* Bloomington, Indiana University Press

Ribadu, Nuhu (2006) *Nigeria's Struggle with Corruption* A Presentation to the US Congressional House Committee on International Development. Washington DC. May 18, 2006

Rosenau, James N. (1969) "Towards the Study of National-International Linkages" in Rosenau, James N. (1969) *Linkage Politics* New York. The Free Press P. 44 - 63

Short, Claire (1999) *Combating Corruption, Promoting Development* London, Department for International Development (DFID)

Sowunmi A, Raufu A. A, Oketokun F. O, Salako M. A, and Usifoh O. O, (2010) *The Role of Media in Curbing Corruption in Nigeria* Research Journal of Information Technology 2(1): 7-23, May 20, 2010

The World Bank (1997) *World Development Report 1997: The State in a Changing World* New York, Oxford University Press

Uhomoibhi, Martin quoted in Adegoroye, Biyi (2011) *Nigeria's National Interest: Foreign Policy Focus* National Mirror June 29, 2012

UNCTAD (2009) *Nigeria: Investment Policy Review.* New York, United Nations Conference on Trade and Development

Chapter Two

LITERATURE REVIEW

This decade is the first to witness the emergence of corruption as a truly global political issue eliciting a global political response

Glynn et al. (1997)

Introduction

In this Chapter, we will conduct a review of the literature in three phases; Corruption and Foreign Policy; Corruption and the Changing Dynamics of Nigerian Foreign Policy; and International Instruments and Conventions for Fighting Corruption.

2.1.0 Corruption and Foreign Policy

Several accounts indicate that both the United States and the former Soviet Union supported corrupt and despotic regimes around the world in order to advance their ideological interests during the Cold War. Mbaku (2000) notes that many corrupt and despotic regimes in Africa including Zaire, South Africa, Liberia, Ethiopia, and Somalia were sustained by the financial and military support they received from the commanding centers of either the capitalist or communist blocs. He observes specifically that the US continued to give development assistance to Zaire – an important ally against the Soviet-backed Angola, even after it became clear that most of the resources were pocketed by President Mobutu Sese Seko and members of his government. Mbaku sums up the link between corruption in the peripheral states and the Cold War policy of the major powers as follows;

> The politics of the Cold War ... contributed significantly
> to the maintenance of a political culture that not only
> condoned corruption but also enhanced the ability of
> incumbent politicians and civil servants to engage in
> political opportunism (Mbaku: 2000: 83).

There has been a substantial paradigm shift in the corruption discourse after the Cold War. Glyn et al (1997) writing under the caption "Globalization of Corruption," notes the transformation of corruption from a predominantly national or regional preoccupation to an issue of global revolutionary force since the 1990s. They observe a huge backlash from corruption scandals erupting in the U.S., France, Italy, Japan, South Korea, India, Pakistan, Mexico, Columbia, South Africa etc., noting that "...this decade is the first to witness the emergence of corruption as a truly global political issue eliciting a global political response."

The authors attribute the corruption eruption to among others, the increasing worldwide availability and consumption of information, the end of the Cold War and the emergence of a truly integrated international economy, and domestic pressures arising from the growth of democracy.

They argue that several factors have led to "globalization" of corruption, such as global economic integration which increases the probability that the effects of corruption will spill over and resonate throughout the world economy. A second factor is the emergence of an electronically networked international financial system that enhances opportunities for corruption, the difficulty of controlling it, and the potential damage it can inflict. Yet, a third factor associated with the phenomenon is the dramatic increase in the number of cooperative strategic alliances, both within countries and across borders in the form of multinational corporations (MNCs)..

The authors trace the roots of international anti-corruption reform to attempts to address the related problem of drug money, including several UN initiatives from the late 1980s, input of the World Economic Forum (The Davos Group), and cross-country research by Transparency International. They also note the impact of the US Foreign Corrupt Practices Act (FCPA), which has influenced the emergence of multilateral anti-corruption regimes in the Organization of American States (OAS), as well as in the Organization for Economic Cooperation and Development (OECD).

Glynn et al (1996) conclude their essay with three important remarks, first is that globalization has drastically altered the nature of corruption. Secondly, the recent changes have not only opened new avenues for corruption, but have also created new conditions that provide unprecedented opportunities for containing or reducing it. Finally, success in the anti-corruption battle requires systematic collaboration and coordination among the authorities of different countries.

By and large, there is some measure of consensus on why there was a world-wide resurgence in the corruption discourse since the 1990s. They include the following:

- End of Cold War policy of supporting corrupt regimes for ideological purposes and the emergence of a truly integrated international economy that is evenly susceptible to the scourge of corruption.
- Increased demand by creditor nations and institutions for transparency and accountability, in the face of non-performing official development assistance (ODA), as an integral part of good governance and sustainable development.
- Revolution in information technology and the parallel expansion of financial services, which simplified the transfer of huge sums of money abroad thereby expanding the scope of fraud, money laundering and corruption (Doig and Theobald: 2000).

Leiken (1996) addresses more directly the harmful effects of corruption on foreign policy, and the use of foreign policy to tackle the problem of corruption. Writing on "Controlling the Corruption Epidemic," Leiken notes that (official corruption) "...represents a hazard to free trade and investment, a threat to democracy and development, and, in collusion with international crime, a danger to national security and public health and safety. Making the critical connection between corruption and foreign policy, he further observes that;

> The hardships of global competition have exhausted voters' patience with government excesses and misconduct. The popular outcry against corruption has activated officials and diplomats already concerned about the harmful effects of crime and bribery on international security and commerce. <u>Consequently corruption is stealing into the precincts of foreign policy.</u> Corruption, money laundering, and drug smuggling have become the subjects of international treaties and assistance programs and now preoccupy international economic organizations as well as intelligence and law enforcement agencies (emphasis mine).

Liken similarly identifies two main sources of the corruption eruption – end of the Cold War accompanied by the rise of civil society; and the spread of democracy and markets, which have increased both the opportunities for graft and the likelihood of exposure. He also notes that 'technological revolution and globalization' are subjecting the political and economic establishments to mistrust and scrutiny.

With respect to the nature of corruption in post-colonial African, Leiken observes that neo-patrimonial regimes are the rule, with emergence of the state as an extension of the ruler's household, in which patronage, ethnic and kinship ties and bribes are the major modes of governance. He attributes the exacerbation of regional, tribal, religious, and ethnic divisions in many African societies, as well as financial hemorrhage in the continent, to corruption-funded patronage to kinsmen and cronies.

In the specific case of Nigeria, Leikan refers to the International Forum for Democratic Studies (IFDS), which estimates that $12.2 billion of governance revenue in the oil-rich country was diverted to "extra-budgetary accounts" between 1988 and 1994, without public accountability. He attributes the irony of fuel scarcity and importation of 70% of petroleum needs in an oil-producing country to the expropriation of funds meant for the construction of oil pipelines, by Nigeria's leaders.

Leiken further notes that while the majority of Nigerians are impoverished, their leaders enrich themselves from oil earnings, which are often stashed away in foreign banks. He notes succinctly that;

> Despite steady oil earnings between 1985 and 1993 – accounting for about 90 per cent of the country's foreign exchange and 80 per cent of its federal revenues – per capita annual gross national product during the period plummeted from $950 to $300

Leiken warns that developing countries are paying a dear price for corruption, in terms of efficiency and credibility. These are manifest in unsafe buildings, bridges, water and air. According to Leiken, corruption undermines trust in government, breeds mutual distrust among citizens and investors, subverts the rule of law, and perverts the work ethic. In short, corruption means that public office is seen as the "road to riches," thereby discouraging productive enterprise.

Leiken suggests modernization of governments, strengthening of civil society, as well as the application of international pressure as different parts of an effective anti-corruption strategy.

2.2.0 Corruption and the Changing Dynamics of Nigeria's Foreign Policy

Perhaps the most comprehensive review of Nigeria's foreign policy during the administration of President Olusegun Obasanjo from both the academic as well as policy standpoints is the international conference organized by the Oxford University's Center for International Studies from 11 to 12 July, 2003. The so-called Oxford Conference dealt with the domestic, regional and external dimensions of Nigeria's foreign policy after the Cold War.

As the official rapporteur to the Conference, Nuamah (2003) summarized papers presented on key issues of the theoretical and practical aspects of Nigeria's foreign policy, the institutions and processes of policy formulation, and the "concentric circles" of domestic, regional and external influences on Nigeria's foreign policy.

The Conference discussed among others, two "faces" that feed into the outcomes of Nigeria's foreign policy process, namely, Nigeria's "fractured" nationhood, and the country's global reputation or "identity" for corruption on its foreign policy. While the Conference conceded that "... the formal institutions of Nigeria's foreign policy are not directly responsible for the limited legitimacy of the state or the widespread perception of Nigeria and Nigerians as corrupt," it acknowledged however, that "... the task of articulating a national interest and representing this interest effectively to the outside world has been seriously affected by both problems."

The Conference gave some useful insights on the subject of corruption and criminality in Nigeria and its impact on the country's international reputation. These include the repercussion of citizens not having the necessary channels to realize their talents and ambitions in Nigeria and the responsibility of government to address the issue of freedom from fear and want for both Nigerians at home and abroad and thus tackle the underlying causes of corruption.

The Conference also noted that part of the problem lies in the way that the international media reports on the issue of corruption in Nigeria, citing "perception" studies by Transparency International, in which participants are asked leading questions such as: "How corrupt do you think Nigeria is on a scale of one to ten?" To the Conference participants, changing the way in which Nigeria is perceived is a necessary imperative if the country is to optimize its foreign policy goals and objectives.

Among the suggestions made by at the Conference, are that active efforts must be made, in conjunction with Nigerian and foreign policy agencies, to apprehend, punish and deter criminal elements who persist in giving Nigeria a bad reputation. Also, the Nigerian government and its overseas diplomatic missions could better access the international media to tell their own story, while the Nigerian media could be given a greater role in mobilizing and motivating the domestic public on critical foreign policy issues.

The presentations made during the Oxford seminar have been compiled into a volume captioned "Gulliver's Trouble: Nigeria's Foreign

Policy after the Cold War" edited by Adebajo, A and Mustapha, A. R. (2008).

In her own contribution to the vexed issue of corruption and Nigeria's international image, Nigeria's Permanent Representative to the United Nations and former Director General of the Nigerian Institute of International Affairs – Professor Joy Ogwu, specifically wrote on Nigeria's national reputation and the logic of rebuilding the country's foreign image. Ogwu (2005) defines the concept of national image as a reflection of the complex relationship between what a nation presents as its foreign policy and its perception by the domestic and external audience. A country's image dwells in the psychological realm and is distinct but nonetheless vital, together with other components of national power including military and economic strength. According to Ogwu;

> A major liability and burden on (Nigeria's) national image is the prevalence of corruption in the society. This has become universally established as a major characteristic of Nigeria in the past two decades.

Nigeria's image as a corrupt country is hinged on several practices prevalent in society, including graft and inflation of contracts, bribery, misappropriation or diversion of funds, kickbacks and over-invoicing, advance fee fraud, notoriously known in Nigeria as '419' and credit cards frauds abroad, among others.

Ogwu cites a study conducted by Shaukat Hassan for the Canadian International Development Agency, in which it was noted that corruption has certain negative consequences for state, including loss of image and prestige, weakening of the moral fiber of the people, lowering of ethical standards in governance and increased social instability and insecurity.

Ogwu however acknowledged steps being taken by the Obasanjo administration to combat the scourge of corruption, including the establishment of two domestic anti-corruption agencies (ACAs) – the Independent Corrupt Practices and other Related Offences Commission (ICPC), as well as the Economic and Financial crimes Commission (EFCC).

Moving outside the (1999 – 2007) timeframe of our studies, the late General Sani Abacha – Nigeria's erstwhile head of State set up the Vision 2010 Committee on November 27, 1996 under the chairmanship of Chief Ernest Shonekan – former head of the Interim National Government (ING), and charged it with the following terms of reference:

- To analyze why Nigeria's national development has been relatively unimpressive in many spheres after more than 36 years of political independence, especially, in relation to its potential;
- to envision where Nigeria would like to be at the time it becomes a fifty-year old independent nation in 2010 and;
- to develop a blueprint and action plans for translating this vision into reality.

The Committee submitted its final report on September 30, 1997 (Shonekan: 1997).

In Chapter 6 of the report captioned "Nigeria's External Image," the Committee defined the external image of any nation as how that nation is perceived by the outside world. It noted that nations strive at all times to have a positive external image, usually inferred from the level of respect and acceptance which they enjoy within the comity of nations and among the nationals of other countries. Such respect and acceptance derive, in turn, from the core values which a nation upholds; the effective management of her domestic affairs and the promotion of her people's interests as well as the conduct of her external relations.

The Committee listed the determinants of the image of a nation as including the following:

- Economic strength;
- Strategic position;
- Management of domestic affairs;
- Military capability;
- Conduct of her citizens abroad;
- Content and effectiveness of her external propaganda;
- Conduct of her diplomatic relations; and
- Circumstances of other countries.

According to the Committee, the goals and objectives of a nation's foreign policy should be guided by the national interest even though it should also be conscious of the advantages of maintaining a good external image. The need then arises to balance the requirements of national interest and the maintenance of a positive external image. Hence, the national interests of a country ultimately revolve round political/diplomatic, socio-economic and military/strategic relations reflecting the domestic circumstances. In this regard, the Committee reinstated the imperative for Nigeria to cultivate international friendship and goodwill.

While noting that the conduct of Nigeria's foreign policy is the statutory responsibility of the Ministry of Foreign Affairs, the Committee acknowledged that Nigeria's external image is also affected by the activities of other agencies of government, non-governmental organizations, the private sector as well as individuals. In a sense, therefore, both the government and the people have an abiding duty in the formulation of policies and actions which portray Nigeria to the best possible light in the international community at all times.

Importantly, the Committee recognizes that there are positive and negative sides to Nigeria's external image. The positive side includes Nigeria's wealth of human and material resources, its relative military and economic advantage in the West African sub-region, as well as its achievements in the field of international football. The negative side of Nigeria's image is the perception by several countries that it has a high degree of corruption manifest in graft and inflation of contracts, advance fee fraud - notoriously known in Nigeria as '419,' credit cards frauds abroad especially in the US, and drug trafficking.

Other negative perceptions of Nigeria, according to the Committee pertain to the lack of good governance with frequent military incursions into government, lack of transparency and accountability at all levels of government, abuse of human rights, high-risk business environment; high incidence of crime and a general insecurity of life and property; and inability to service her external debt or honor other obligations as and when due.

The Committee outlines some of the consequences of Nigeria's poor external image, as including the declining flow of foreign direct investment into the country; divestment from Nigeria; a gradual alienation from Nigeria's traditional friends; harassment of Nigerians in foreign countries by such local agencies as immigration, customs and the police, mostly on unwarranted suspicion; suspension from The Commonwealth; and the devaluation of Nigerian educational system and the consequential increasing non-acceptance of Nigerian academic qualifications.

The Committee further classified the major problems affecting Nigeria's external image into three areas: socio-political, economic, and diplomatic. Among the socio-political problems are the high incidence of fraud; the high level of corruption; the lack of a culture of commitment, integrity and excellence; and the high incidence of involvement in drug trafficking.

The Committee notes that the restoration of Nigeria's external image requires the collaborative efforts of all stakeholders, organizations, government agencies, Non-Governmental Organizations (NGOs) and the private sector at bilateral and multilateral levels. The Committee further noted that the external image of a country is always a reflection of her domestic state of affairs, and Nigeria's efforts should, therefore, be concentrated on getting the fundamentals at home right, while managing her external relations more effectively.

The Shonekan-led Vision 2010 Committee suggested that in order for Nigeria to restore and sustain a positive external image, it should strive to establish and sustain good and stable governance; achieve rapid and sustained economic growth and development; play increasing leadership role in Africa's political and economic development and security arrangements; effectively manage its external debt portfolio; and effectively manage its diplomatic relations.

Still on the domestic challenge of corruption and Nigeria's image, the Kaduna State Government, in conjunction with the New Nigerian Newspapers Limited and the Nigerian Television Authority organized a seminar on the Appraisal of the Social and Moral Image of the Nigerian Society from 7th – 9th June 1995 at Kaduna. The objective of the Seminar was to identify, discuss and proffer solutions to Nigeria's socio-economic and political difficulties and the crisis of a bad image abroad, and markedly captioned "Not in Our Character" (Isa: 1995).

A total of 13 papers were presented on important aspects of national life including the Mass Media, Human Rights, democratization, Conflict Resolution, Social and Moral Values, Political Stability and the Politics of Drug Trafficking.

On the issue of the Media and Nigerian Image, the Seminar acknowledged the existence of many activities in which Nigerians are engaged in, often in collaboration with foreigners, which have worked to create a negative image for such Nigerians. But it rejected the notion that Nigeria is a nation of corrupt and dangerous people as was being propagated by the Western media. Chief Walter Ofonagoro – the erstwhile Minister of Information during the Abacha regime enumerated some of the specific negative media portrayal of Nigeria as follows:

- Eighty percent of all hard drugs consumed in the United States come from Nigeria.
- Nigeria controls forty two and a half percent of all organized crime business in the world, including the home-grown Advance Fee Fraud (AFF) popularly known as "419."
- Ninety percent of Nigerian marriages contracted in Britain are fraudulent.
- Military regime in Nigeria was abusing human rights including a clamp down on journalists, media organizations, and civil rights groups,
- Chief M. K. O. Abiola, the purported winner of the June 12 presidential election was denied his mandate and put in jail.
- Nigeria earned over $200 billion from years of oil production, but has nothing to show for it, except a very low per capita and a huge foreign debt.

In his contribution to the Seminar, Alhaji Adamu Ciroma – one time Governor of the Central Bank of Nigeria, lamented the international absurdities that Nigeria and Nigerian were subjected to, including the rough and unpleasant treatment Nigerians received from the customs and security officials of other countries based on the general assumption that all Nigerians were crooks, and consequently, the shifting of focus in economic events in Africa from Nigeria to other countries like Uganda, Kenya, and Ghana. He lamented the condemnation of Nigeria's record by the International Human Rights Conference in Norway, and the shifting of the venue of the Coca-Cola international football tournament from Nigeria to Qatar on flimsy grounds. Ciroma further cited Nigeria's inability to meet its international financial obligations as a result of the "poor and dishonest management of the economy, as contributing to the portrayal of Nigeria as a rogue nation.

Another speaker at the Seminar, Professor Alkali drew attention to "another World War which is going on silently, and which has already brought down many nations." Unlike the First and Second World Wars, the present war, according to the Professor, is not fought with guns and tanks, but "with tongues and through the media," and the objective of this psychological war waged against many developing nations, is to;

> Create bad international image for (the) targeted countries, to kill the morale of their leaders and followers, (and) to create tension and state of insecurity.

The Seminar in its Communique recommended that Government should more actively challenge and counteract the negative effects of such propaganda. The Seminar also noted the severe decline in the levels of social and moral value which feed the political and economic life of the country. It noted in particular, the widespread concern of Nigerians over current rates of social disintegration, economic polarization, corruption, and crime, and youth delinquency, further acknowledging that these problems were exacerbated by economic hardships which affect the vast majority of Nigerians.

The Seminar attributed the creation of such crimes as corruption and international drug-trafficking, in which some Nigerian were involved, to the rapid changes in international communication systems. It commended steps taken by the Abacha regime to address these problems through the enactment of drastic legislation against drug trafficking, money laundering, and advance fee fraud or "419," and appealed to the wider public to extend its support to law enforcement agencies to identify and arrest drug traffickers.

The Chairman of the Independent National Electoral Commission (INEC) – Professor Attahiru Jega, clearly indicts corruption among other factors, as being responsible for the continued under-performance of Nigeria's foreign policy in contemporary times. Jega (2010) maintains that Nigeria has come a long way in international relations, from the immediate post-independence era of the 1960s to the first decade of the new millennium when Nigeria is well known, unfortunately, due more to the dubious distinction of its citizens involvement in global crimes, ranging from "drug-trafficking to fraud (419) and now terrorism."

Writing under the caption, "Nigeria's Foreign Policy and the Promotion of Peace, Development, and Democracy," Jega attributes Nigeria's growing frustration in the actualization of its coveted leadership role in Africa, to the link between domestic processes and the conduct of foreign policy. According to Jega (2010);

> Weak economic and political structures, ineffective institutions and processes, and bad governance, characterized by quarrelsome, inept and corrupt public officers, have combined to undermine, except for a brief period (1975 – 1979), the influence and respectability that ought to have accrued to Nigeria's foreign policy undertakings in the past fifty years.

He further explains the contradiction of being a rich country with very poor people in terms of the recklessness of greedy and self-serving Nigerian elite who have mismanaged the economy, undermined infrastructure and socio-economic development, and basically squirreled away the country's resources into their private coffers. A domestic environment that is characterized by insecurity, poverty, ethno-religious mobilization, and youth unemployment has negatively constrained and influenced or otherwise conditioned the making and execution of Nigeria's foreign policy.

Jega surmises that Nigeria's leadership status in Africa is rather presumptuous as many phrases have emerged to describe Nigeria, in relationship to the rest of the world as, 'a crippled giant,' 'an open sore of the continent,' 'a giant with clay feet,' etc.

2.3.0 International Instruments and Conventions for Fighting Corruption

Various instruments and treaties have been developed for the purpose of combating corruption at various levels (United Nations: 2005). At the global and inter-regional level are the respective United Nations Convention against Corruption (UNCAC); United Nations Convention against Transnational Organized Crime (UNTOC), as well as the OECD Convention on the Bribery of Foreign Public Officials in International Business Transactions. Africa has the respective African Union Convention on Preventing and Combating Corruption; SADC Protocol against Corruption, as well as the ECOWAS Protocol against Corruption. The Inter-American Convention against Corruption is in operation in the Americas, while the ADB-OECD Action Plan for Asia-Pacific applies to Asia. Europe has the respective Council of Europe Criminal Law, and Council of Europe Criminal Law. A closer look at some of these conventions is next in order.

2.3.1 United Nations Convention against Corruption (UNCAC)

The United Nations Convention against Corruption was adopted by the General Assembly of the United Nations on 31 October 2003 at its Headquarters in New York. The Convention entered into force on 14 December 2005, with 140 signatories and 95 ratifications/accessions as at 20 August 2007. This is in accordance with article 68 (1) which provides that;

> This Convention shall enter into force on the ninetieth day after the date of deposit of the thirtieth instrument of ratification, acceptance, approval or accession.

The Preamble to the Convention notes, among others, the threat that corruption poses to economic development, political stability and the due process of law. It also acknowledges the transnational nature of corruption, hence the need for international cooperation in combating it. It further recalls previous multilateral treaties in the field, including the Africa Union Convention on Preventing and Combating Corruption 2003.

The main body of the Convention is divided into eight chapters and 71 articles. Chapter one contains the general provisions of the Convention. Article 1 (a) of Chapter 1 outlines the purpose of the Convention which is, among others;

> To promote and strengthen measures to prevent and combat corruption more efficiently and effectively.

Chapter two deals with preventive measures, which include the establishment of national anti-corruption bodies and public sector reforms such as code of conduct for public officials and public procurement reforms. Provisions are also made for preventive measures in the private sector as well as participation of the society and measures to prevent money laundering.

Chapter three deals with criminalization and law enforcement, and takes steps to criminalize such actions as bribery of national and intergovernmental public officials, embezzlement, misappropriation, and illicit enrichment. Such actions also extend to the private sector. The chapter also provides for freezing, seizure and confiscation of proceeds of corruption and deals with the issues of jurisdiction as well as international cooperation in criminal prosecution.

Chapter four provides specifically for international cooperation, including the areas of extradition, mutual legal assistance and law enforcement cooperation. Chapter five dwells on assets recovery. Chapter six deals with technical assistance and information exchange. Chapter outlines mechanisms for implementation of the Convention, while chapter eight contains final provisions on such issues as implementation and entry into force of the Convention.

2.3.2 African Union Convention on Preventing and Combating Corruption

The AU Convention on Preventing and Combating Corruption was adopted by Heads of State and Governments of the Africa Union at their Summit in Maputo, Mozambique, on 12 July 2003 and entered into force on 5 August 2006.

The preamble to the 28-article Convention among others, expresses concern about the negative effect of corruption on the political, economic, social and cultural development of Africa, and recognizes the need to address the root causes of corruption through partnership between governments and all segments of the society.

Article 1 of the Convention deals with definition of terms, while article 2 states the objectives of the Convention which include to:

> Promote and strengthen the development in Africa by each State Party of mechanisms required to prevent, detect, punish and eradicate corruption and related offences in the public and private sectors.

Article 3 deals with the principles of the Convention which include transparency and accountability in the management of public affairs, and condemnation of acts of corruption.

Article 4 defines the scope of application of the Convention. It covers solicitation or acceptance, offering or granting, acts or omission, and diversion, in connection with corruption, illicit enrichment, as well as acts of collusion between State Parties. Article 5 sets out legislative and other measures to be adopted by State Parties including independent anticorruption agencies, public sector reforms, protection of informants and witnesses, and school education programmes. Article 6 covers laundering of the proceeds of corruption. It enjoins State Parties to take steps to criminalize the conversion, transfer or disposal of illicit property within its territory.

The fight against corruption and related offences in the public service is detailed in Article 7, and includes provisions for declaration of assets and code of conduct. It also provides that the immunity granted to some public officials shall not be an obstacle to the investigation and prosecution of suspects, subject however to national legislations. Article 8 provides for the offence of illicit enrichment, while article 9 guarantees access to information. Article 10 provides for transparency in the funding of political parties, article 11 extends the fight against corruption to the private sector, while article 12 incorporates the civil society and media as well.

Article 13 deals with jurisdiction, article 14 provides minimum guarantees of a fair trial, and article 16 deals with confiscation and seizure of the proceeds and instrumentalities of corruption, including the repatriation of proceeds of corruption. Article 17 provides for bank secrecy, enjoining State Parties not to invoke bank secrecy to deny any requests made pursuant to the provisions of the Convention. Article 18 provides for cooperation and mutual legal assistance among State Parties to prevent, detect, investigate and punish acts of corruption, while article 19 provides for wider international cooperation in the fight against corruption.

Article 20 provides for national authorities to act as liaisons for the purpose of effecting the provisions of the Convention. Article 21 provides for supremacy of the Convention in relationship with other agreements dealing with corruption. Articles 23, 24, 25, 26, 27, and 28 contain the final provisions of the Convention. They include such formalities as signatures, reservations, amendment, denunciation etc.

2.3.3 ECOWAS Protocol on the Fight against Corruption

The Economic Community of West Africa (ECOWAS) Protocol on the Fight against Corruption was signed on December 21, 2001. The Protocol has a total of 27 articles. Article 2 outlines the three aims and objectives of the Protocol, viz:

i)   To promote and strengthen the development in each of the State Parties effective mechanisms to prevent, suppress and eradicate corruption;

ii) To intensify and revitalize cooperation between State Parties, with a view to making anti-corruption measures more effective; and

iii) To promote the harmonization and coordination of national anticorruption laws and policies.

Accordingly, Articles 3 and 4 deal with scope and jurisdiction respectively while article 5 lists preventive measures which States Parties are expected to take, including national laws, ethical guidelines and codes of conduct. Other preventive measures include procurement laws, whistleblower protection, participation of CSOs and NGOs, revenue laws, declaration of assets by public officials, domestic anticorruption agencies (ACAs) and press freedom.

Article 6 of the Protocol outlines what constitutes acts of corruption including the demand, or offering of pecuniary gifts by public officials directly or indirectly, in exchange for certain acts or omission or promises therefore conferring undue advantage. Acts of corruption as defined under the Protocol also include diversion of public goods, unaccounted wealth, over invoicing, bribery and other forms of illicit enrichment. Article 7 provides for the laundering of proceeds of corruption and similar criminal offences. Article 8 provides for the protection of witnesses, while Article 9 contains provision for assistance and protection of victims.

Article 10 provides for sanctions and measures to be applied by State Parties for infractions of the Protocol, while Article 11 provides for liability of legal persons, including criminal, civil or administrative liabilities. Liabilities may involve monetary sanctions, disqualification from commercial activities, judicial winding-up orders, and placements under judicial supervision.

Article 12 deals with acts of corruption concerning foreign public officials, while Article 13 contains provisions for seizures and forfeiture of the proceeds of crime. Article 14 makes offenders under the Protocol subject to extradition. Article 15 provides for mutual legal assistance and law enforcement cooperation between the State Parties relating to the investigation and prosecution of acts of corruption. Article 16 obliges the State Parties to designate a Central Authority for the purpose of mutual legal assistance and cooperation.

Article 17 provides for application of time in respect of offences committed before the Protocol came into force, while Article 18 urges State Parties to work towards harmonizing their national laws for the purpose of realizing the objectives of the Protocol. Article 19 provides for the establishment of a technical commission to be known as the Anti-corruption Commission, with specific objectives.

Article 20 provides for the relationship of the Protocol with other treaties. Article 22 provides for ratification and entry into force of the Protocol, upon ratification by at least nine (9) signatory States. Article 23 provides for the depository authority and registration of the Protocol instrument with the ECOWAS Executive Secretariate. Article 24 provides for accession to the Protocol by non-ECOWAS member states.

Article 25 contains provision for amendments and revision of the Protocol by the State Parties. Article 26 provides for denunciation of the Protocol by State Parties, while Article 27 contains provisions for settlement of disputes between State Parties to the Protocol by the ECOWAS Court of Justice.

References
Chapter Two

Adebajo, Adekeye and Mustapha, Abdul Raufu (2008) *Gulliver's Troubles: Nigeria's Foreign Policy after the Cold War* South Africa, University of KwaZulu-Natal Press

Doig, Alan and Theobald, Robin (2000) "Why Corruption?" in Doig, Alan and Theobald, Robin Eds. (2000) *Corruption and Democratization* London, Frank Cass

Glynn Patrick, Kobrin Stephen J, Naim Moises (1997) *The Globalization of Corruption* Institute for International Economics http://www.iie.com

Isa, Lawal J. (Ed) (1995) *Not in Our Character: Proceeding of the National Seminar on the Appraisal of the Social and Moral Image of the Nigerian Society* Kaduna, Kaduna State Government

Jega, Attahiru M. (2010) "Nigeria's Foreign Policy and the Promotion of Peace, Development, and Democracy," in Jega, Attahiru M. and Farris, Jacqueline W. (Eds.) (2010) *Nigeria at Fifty: Contributions to Peace, Democracy and Development* Abuja, The Shehu Musa Yar'Adua Foundation

Leiken, Robert S. (1996) *Controlling the Global Corruption Epidemic* Foreign Policy No. 105 (Winter, 1996-1997) Pp. 55 – 73.

Mbaku, John M. (2000) *Bureaucratic and Political Corruption in Africa: the Public Choice Perspective* Florida, Krieger Publishing Company

Nuamah, Rosemary (Rpt) (2003) *Nigeria's Foreign Policy after the Cold War: Domestic, Regional and External Influences* Oxford, University of Oxford.

Ogwu, Joy (2005) *National Reputation and the Logic of Rebuilding Nigeria's Foreign Image* The Guardian October 20, 2005 Page 8

Shonekan, E. A. O. (1997) *Vision 2010 Committee Vol. 1 Main Report* Abuja, The Presidency

United Nations (2005) *Compendium of International Legal Instruments on Corruption 2nd Edition* New York, United Nations

Chapter Three

CORRUPTION AND FOREIGN POLICY IN NIGERIA: A HISTORICAL PERSPECTIVE

> Just as some of us stood against apartheid and won. Just as some of us stood against colonialism and won...fought the military and won. Fighting for good governance and fighting corruption has to be done by us...Fighting corruption is far more difficult than all the other difficulties we have faced.
>
> Nuhu Ribadu (From exile).

Introduction

In this Chapter, we will examine the interaction between corruption and Nigerian foreign policy in a historical perspective. For ease of presentation, we will present our discussion in three segments – Corruption and Nigerian Foreign Policy in the First Republic (1960 – 1966); Corruption and Nigerian Foreign Policy in the Second Republic (1979 – 1983); and Corruption and Nigerian Foreign Policy under Military Rule.

3.1.0 Corruption and Nigerian Foreign Policy in the First Republic (1960 – 1966)

Alhaji Abubakar Tafawa Balewa – Nigeria's first Prime Minister and head of government articulated and enunciated the fundamental principles underpinning the country's external relations in three major speeches, namely, his statement in the House of Representatives on August 20, 1960; his Independence Day address on October 1, 1960;

44

and his acceptance speech on the occasion of Nigeria's accession to membership of the United Nations in New York on October 8, 1960.

The broad principles of Nigeria's foreign policy as laid out by Alhaji Tafawa Balewa have been summarized as follows:

- Promotion of the national interest of the federation and of its citizens;
- Nonalignment with any of the then existing ideological and military power blocs, especially NATO and the Warsaw Pact;
- Respect for the legal equality, political independence, sovereignty and territorial integrity of all states;
- Respect for the doctrine of non-interference in the domestic affairs of all other states;
- Seeking membership of both continental and global multilateral organizations for their functional importance to Nigeria; and
- That Africa would be the cornerstone of the country's external relations.

These precepts as laudable as they were at the time were however subject to the vagaries and dynamics of domestic circumstances and world politics. However, the core foreign policy issues that the First Republic had to deal with includes the Congo crisis, the Anglo-Nigerian Defence Pact, Commonwealth relations and UN membership, the question of "two Chinas", the Arab-Israeli conflict, the decolonization of Southern Africa and the Portuguese speaking African territories, Apartheid in South Africa and negotiations with the European Economic Community (Adeniran: 1985). Nigeria's foreign policy in the First Republic has however been described as conservative and timid (Osaghae: 1998).

Corruption in Nigeria predates the country's independence, and has been traced to the colonial public service between 1945 and 1960. Falola (1998: 138) notes a concern expressed by the Governor of Lagos in 1946 as follows:

> One of the curses of this country (is) bribery and until there exist a national conscience which will condemn

the practice and an individual one which will neither
offer nor accept bribe, no real progress can be made.

Falola identified three prevalent forms of corruption in colonial
Nigeria - bribery, misappropriation, and nepotism, and attributed
corruption during this period to among other factors, lack of commitment
to the colonial state by public servants, conditions of extreme poverty
and inequality, and ineffective laws.

Several foremost Nigerian nationalists were indicted for corrupt
practices beginning from the 1950s when the first panel of inquiry
was set up to look into African Continental Bank (ACB). The charges
were that Dr. Azikiwe abused his office by allowing public funds to
be invested in the bank, in which he had an interest. The allegation
was investigated by the Justice Strafford Forster-Sutton Commission of
enquiry set up on July 24, 1956. The Commission's Report of January 6,
1957 indicted Dr. Azikiwe, and he subsequently transferred his rights
and interest in the bank to the Government of Eastern Nigeria.

Similarly, in June 1962 the Federal Government appointed a
Commission headed by Justice G. B. Coker to investigate the relationship
between the Chief Obafemi Awolowo – led Western Regional
Government and the National Investment and Property Company. The
Coker Commission found Chief Awolowo guilty of misuse of Western
regional funds – specifically, that he diverted funds from the regional
government-owned Corporation, totaling N4.4 million in cash and
N1.3 million in overdraft, from the National Bank (also owned by
the Western region) to finance the Action Group (AG) and publish
newspapers supporting the party – and indicted him for trying to build
a financial empire through abuse of his official position (Osaghae: 1998).

In providing a background to Nigerian's First Republic, Izah (1991)
traced the internal problems of "regionalism, tribalism, nepotism and
corruption" as accounting for much of the economic and political
weakness of the Republic, which robbed it of a strong and virile foreign
policy and eventually led to its downfall.

Major Chukwuma Kaduna Nzeogwu and his colleagues harped on
the theme of corruption when they overthrew the Government of the
First Republic in a bloody military coup;

Our enemies are the political profiteers, the swindlers, the men in high and low places that seek bribes and demand 10 percent; those that seek to keep the country divided permanently so that they can remain in office as ministers or VIPs of waste; the tribalists, the nepotists, those that make the country look big for nothing before international circles, those that have corrupted our society and put the Nigerian political calendar back by their words and deeds (Nzeogwu: 1966).

General Aguiyi-Ironsi who took over government after Major Nzeogwu's failed coup committed his regime to correcting some of the anomalies of the First Republic including eradication of tribalism, corruption and dishonesty in public life. He instituted commissions of enquiry into some major parastatals such as the Electricity Corporation of Nigeria, Nigeria Railway Corporation, the Nigerian Ports Authority, and the notoriously corrupt Lagos City Council (Osaghae: 1998).

3.2.0 Corruption and Nigerian Foreign Policy in the Second Republic (1979 – 1983)

Alhaji Shehu Shagari was sworn in as the first democratically elected Executive President of Nigeria on October 1, 1979. President Shagari outlined the principles of his administration's foreign policy during his maiden speech, which includes the following:

- Africa shall remain the cornerstone of Nigeria's foreign policy.
- Africa shall be free, free of racial bigotry, free of oppression, and free from the vestiges of colonialism.
- Support for the United Nations, the Organization of African Unity, the Economic Community of West African States, and the Organization of Petroleum Exporting Countries.
- Enhancement of the cause of peace, prosperity and progress through mutual respect and co-operation between nations.

The Shehu Shagari administration attached great importance to the fight against apartheid and decolonization in Southern Africa making yearly allocation of $5 million to aid the liberation movements in southern Africa, but the administration's foreign policy approach is described as being lackluster and devoid of the dynamism of the previous Mohammed/Obasanjo regime. Shagari's foreign policy shortcomings include his futile attempts to keep the peace in Chad, his seeming impotence in dealing with the conflict with Cameroon over the Bakassi Peninsula dispute, and the expulsion of illegal aliens from Nigeria.

Generally, the four years of Shagari's administration is described as a period of recess for Nigeria's foreign policy and was marked by a conservative and cautious approach (Osaghae: 1998). The shortcomings in President Shagari's foreign policy is attributed to among other factors, constraints associated with the democratic republican constitution under which he operated, and economic crisis in the country which became evident by 1981 (Uzoigwe et al: 2004).

On the anti-corruption front, the fifth schedule of the 1979 Constitution provides for a Code of Conduct for Public officials which among others, prohibited public officials from engaging in activities that could lead to a conflict between their personal interest and official duty; they were precluded from engaging in private business, from seeking or accepting gifts or benefits in the executing of their duties. Certain categories of public officials were also prohibited from operating foreign accounts and were required to declare their assets at intervals. A Code of Conduct Tribunal was set up to try and punish erring officials.

Notwithstanding, the Shagari administration squandered the national treasury to the extent that it had to enforce domestic belt-tightening measures called the Economic Stabilization Act from April 1982 and later had to seek an IMF loan facility of about $2.2 billion to bail it out. The economy had been wrecked by squandermania, wanton official corruption and greed, in the face of dwindling oil revenues that was occasioned by the global oil glut of the early 1980s. Between 1979 and 1983, Nigeria earned about N40.5 billion and squandered it. The external reserve of N2.3 billion, she inherited in 1979 was wiped out and replaced with a staggering external debt of N10.21 billion.

According to Nwachuku (2004);

> Government contracts were inflated to support
> kickbacks, imports were over invoiced, forgery and
> fraud were rampant, officials embezzled public funds
> and no effective measures were taken against smuggling.

A typical example of inflation of contracts during the Shagari administration was the £300 million British Aerospace contract for the supply of eighteen Jaguar jets, from which NPN stalwarts were said to have received 'kickbacks' of £22 million (Osaghae: 1998).

The life of the Shagari civilian administration was terminated on 31st December 1983, paving way for Buhari/Idiagbon military administration. In his coup speech of January 1, 1984, General Muhammadu Buhari remarked as follows:

> While corruption and indiscipline have been associated
> with our state of under-development, these two evils in
> our body politic have attained unprecedented height in
> the past few years. The corrupt, inept and insensitive
> leadership in the last four years has been the source
> of immorality and impropriety in our society. Arson
> has been used to cover up fraudulent acts in public
> institutions. Corruption has become so pervasive and
> intractable that a whole ministry has been created to
> stem it.

He made it clear that his government will not tolerate kick-backs, inflation of contracts and over-invoicing of imports etc. Nor will it condone forgery, fraud, embezzlement, misuse and abuse of office and illegal dealings in foreign exchange and smuggling. He re-stated his resolve to see that corrupt officials and their agents will be brought to book.

Consequently, politicians were held under the State Security (Detention of Persons) Decree No. 2 of 1984 and many were tried by the Recovery of Public Property Special Military Tribunals established by Decree No. 3. Some were convicted for various offences and duly sentenced. Specifically, the Justice Mohammed Bello Tribunal convicted 51 politicians and placed refund orders on them for their ill-gotten wealth. Many state governors were found in possession of large sums of money when the army took over the government.

The level of corruption during the Second Republic continued to resonate even after the overthrow of the succeeding Buhari's regime. General Babangida who, in turn, overthrew General Buhari noted in his maiden speech of August 27, 1985 that "The history of our nation had never recorded the degree of indiscipline and corruption as in the period between October 1979 and December 1983."

3.3.0 Corruption and Nigerian Foreign Policy under Military Rule

This section of the historical perspective on corruption and Nigerian foreign policy under military rule covers the respective regimes of General Yakubu Gowon (1966 – 1975); Generals Murtala Muhammed/ Olusegun Obasanjo (1975 – 1979); Generals Muhammadu Buhari/ Tunde Idiagbo (1984 – 1985); General Ibrahim Babangida (1985 – 1993); General Sani Abacha (1993 – 1998); and General Abdulsalaami Abubakar (1998 – 1999).

3.3.1 General Yakubu Gowon (1966 – 1975)

Major Nzeogwu, General Ironsi, and Lt. Col (later General) Gowon each affirmed adherence to the foreign policy objectives and commitments of the First Republic. However, only General Gowon stayed in office long enough to make any meaningful impact on Nigerian foreign policy in the face of the domestic political instability and national uncertainty at the time. The main foreign policy thrust and exertions of Gowon's regime were dictated by domestic constraints of the civil war (1967 – 1970), hence;

Nigeria broke diplomatic relations with Gabon, the Ivory Coast, Tanzania, and Zambia for recognizing secessionist Biafra, had strained relations with France and hostility toward Israel for having Biafran sympathies, became "cool" towards Britain and the United States for not actively supporting the Federal Government's war efforts, and established stronger ties with the Soviet Union and Egypt as a result of the assistance they gave to the Federal Government (Adeniran: 1985).

The direction of Nigeria's foreign policy in the immediate post-civil war years also drew from the country's experiences during the war;

It sharpened Nigeria's perception of national security and survival, the importance of good neighbors, the need for diversification of external relations and proper nonalignment, the need for economic integration, African unity and the seriousness of the anti-colonial and anti-apartheid struggle on the African continent (Fawole: 2003: 54)

In practical terms, Gowon's regime continued making payments to the Liberation Committee of the OAU as well as being vociferous in its condemnation of Apartheid and its supporters. Nigeria spearheaded the campaign against the Anglo-Rhodesian settlement scheme in Zimbabwe in 1971, recognized Communist China and embarked on reconciliation with pro-Biafran African states, while assuming chairmanship of the OAU in 1973. General Gowon was part of the failed African Peace Mission to the Middle East, and economic negotiations with Europe was on top gear through the EEC (Adeniran: 1985). The formation of ECOWAS in July 1975 was probably the greatest foreign policy feat of the Gowon administration.

The discovery of oil and soaring prices in the early 1970s not only added fillip to the ability of the Gowon regime to vigorously pursue its foreign policy pronouncement, but also laid the basis for much of the corruption that was to pervade both his regime and subsequent administrations in the country. According to Metz (1991);

> Graft, bribery, and nepotism (became) an integral part of a complex system of patronage and "gift" giving through which influence and authority were asserted.

Part of Gowon's nine-point program unveiled on the occasion of Nigeria's 10th national independence anniversary was "eradication of corruption in the national life," and in 1973 the regime established a special anticorruption police force--the "X-Squad" - whose subsequent investigations revealed wide-spread corruption not only in government and public corporations but also in private business as well as in some professional bodies. The importation of expired drugs and inferior building/road construction materials often at inflated costs were part of scandals, which extended to even hospitals and orphanages. In the majority of cases, the culprits were a combination of Nigerian businessmen, government officials, and foreign companies.

Gowon's regime especially the state governors and public servants was continually dogged by allegations of economic mismanagement, corruption, extravagance and inequality. The open allegations of corruption made against Joseph Tarka – the Federal Minister of Communications and Joseph Gomwalk – the Governor of Benue-Plateau State were instructive in this regard. Gowon's seeming inability to discipline the erring officials was to contribute to public outrage and indignation against his administration (Njoku: 2004).

General Gowon's conservative approach and his conciliatory attitude towards governance is said to have contributed to corruption in his administration; According to Fawole (2003:55), Gowon's personal attitude towards governance;

> ...turned out to become a severe leadership weakness when he could not remove or even redeploy his military governors in the face of allegations of corruption against them.

By March 1974, the Ministry of Defence was involved in a cement importation scandal in which the cost of purchase and freight of 2.9 metric tons of cement was inflated by nearly 100% from $40 per ton to $75. The Justice M. B. Belgore Panel set up by government to investigate the alleged irregularity indicted the permanent secretary and other officials of the Ministry of Defence. But even though the indicted officials were removed from office, no criminal charges were brought against them (Chukwudum: 2000).

The report of a three-man panel set up by the succeeding regime of General Murtala Muhhamed to examine the assets of former military governors, the former administrator of the East Central State and some former federal commissioners, found that nine out of eleven former military governors grossly abused their office, and they were made to forfeit assets worth over ten million naira to the State (Chuku: 2004). The profligacy of the Gowon regime in an era of oil boom left Nigeria with a debt burden of $1.6 billion.

3.3.2 Murtala Muhammed/Olusegun Obasanjo (1975 – 1979)

General Murtala Mohammed came into power in a military coup in July 1975, with General Olusegun Obasanjo as his second-in-command. General Mohammed indicated the general direction of his regime's foreign policy in his maiden speech of July 29, 1975 as follows:

> (Finally,) we reaffirm this country's friendship with all countries. Foreign nationals living in Nigeria will be protected. Foreign investments will also be protected. The government will honour all obligations entered into by the previous Governments of the Federation. We will also give continued support to the Organization of African Unity, the United Nations Organization, and the Commonwealth.

From August 1975 until his death in February 1976, General Mohammed took some radical measures which enjoyed popular support at home, endeared Nigeria to progressive African countries, and impressed other nations interested in the true liberation of Africa (Adeniran: 1985). His regime increased Nigeria's material and financial contributions to the liberation movements in Southern Africa, and granted recognition to MPLA as the legitimate government of Angola.

Following General Mohammed's death in a bloody coup attempt on February 13, 1976, General Obasanjo continued the domestic and foreign policies initiated by the duo at inception in 1975. General Obasanjo outlined his regime's foreign policy as follows:

- The defence of Nigeria's sovereignty, independence and territorial integrity.
- The defence of the independence and territorial integrity of all African countries, and the fostering of national self-reliance, and rapid economic development.
- The promotion of equality and self-reliance in Africa and the rest of the developing world.
- The promotion and defence of justice and respect for human dignity.
- The defence and promotion of world peace.

The most notable foreign policy outings of the Obasanjo regime include increased support for the Patriotic Front of Zimbabwe and the subsequent condemnation of the Anglo-American peace proposals, the nationalization of the British Petroleum, contribution to the historic London Conference on Zimbabwe, and mediation in the Chadian and Western Sahara conflicts (Adeniran: 1985).

Also known as the golden age of Nigeria's foreign policy, the duo of Muhammed and Obasanjo stamped their authority boldly on Nigeria's foreign policy recording a number of foreign policy successes and achievements. The military's peculiar authoritarian decision-making style permitted them to have their ways and impose their own visions on the country. The regime's foreign policy thrust was buoyed by among others, the relative advantages that Nigeria enjoyed in Africa in terms of population (one in every four Black African was a Nigerian), it's booming oil-based economy, a large army and a robust military budget (Table 3.1).

Table 3.1 Nigeria/Africa Statistics 1975 (%)

	Nigeria		
	Africa	Sub-Sahara	ECOWAS
Population	17.5	22	58.4
GNP	16.3	23.6	63.1
Army		66.9	76.2
Military Expenditure		42.7	81.8

Source: Fawole (2003)

The Muhammed/Obasanjo regime adopted an orchestrated strategy for the fight against corruption. Panels set up to probe former state military governors and top government officials in the Gowon regime, found massive corruption mostly involving embezzlement of public funds, which resulted in the seizure of stolen assets valued at over ten million naira. Over 10,000 public officials were "purged" from the civil service for various reasons including fraud and corrupt practices. The regime further created anti-corruption institutions, notably the Assets Investigation Panel, Corrupt Practices Investigation Bureau, and Special Anti-Corruption Tribunal, as well as promulgation of Decree No. 38 – Corrupt Practices Decree 1975.

As part of the regime's "low profile" policy and leadership by example, public officers including the head of state and members of the Supreme Military Council were directed to declare their assets, of which illegitimate excesses were to be forfeited to government. But these measures were not sufficient to stamp out corruption from the polity. Obarogie Ohonbamu – a lecturer at the University of Lagos, accused the head of state of under-declaring his assets, and was subsequently detained under the Public Officers (Protection against False Accusation) Decree of 1976.

The major reason for the failure of the Muhammad/Obasanjo regime's anticorruption war, as adduced by Nwachuku (2004) is that "...those in a position to implement the anti-corruption measures were themselves the symbols of corruption." Beginning from 1977, the Federal Government resorted to heavy borrowing from the Western money market, without taming its own economy or controlling the drain pipe which ECOWAS had become.

The Justice Ayo Irikefe Panel set up by Alhaji Shehu Shagari to probe N2.8 billion missing from NNPC accounts during General Obasanjo's regime found the money lodged with the London branch of Bank of Credit and Commerce International (BCCI) but interests accumulated on the money between 1977 and 1980 was never credited to Nigeria. Alhaji Dasuki and late Shehu Musa Yaradua were particularly close to BCCI banking conglomerate, and presided over the opening of the BCCI branch in Nigeria.

3.3.3 General Muhammadu Buhari/General Tunde Idiagbon (1984 – 1985)

The first major foreign policy issue that the new Buhari regime had to deal with after it overthrew the civilian administration of President Shehu Shagari on 31st December 1983 stemmed from the domestic polity i.e., revamping the ailing economy, in what became known as the policy of economic nationalism. Profligacy of the Second Republic politicians especially misuse of power by the law-makers was largely responsible for transforming Nigeria into a debtor nation (Agedah; 1993).

In his coup speech of January 1, 1984 General Buhari clarified the direction of his regime's foreign policy as follows:

> Our foreign policy will both be dynamic and realistic. Africa will of course continue to be the centre piece of our foreign policy. The Federal Military Government will maintain and strengthen existing diplomatic relations with other states and with international organisations and institutions such as the Organisation of African

Unity, the United Nations and its organs, Organisation
of Petroleum Exporting Countries, ECOWAS and the
Commonwealth etc. The Federal Military Government
will honour and respect all treaties and obligations
entered into by the previous government and we hope
that such nations and bodies will reciprocate this
gesture by respecting our country's territorial integrity
and sovereignty.

Buhari's Afro-centric foreign policy was exemplified by the attention
he paid to the issue of the struggle for the independence of Namibia, and
particularly to the dismantling of apartheid in South Africa. However,
Anglo-Nigerian relations suffered setbacks from the beginning because
Britain was seen as harboring many Nigerian politicians who were
accused of looting the national treasury and refusing to cooperate in
their extradition. In July 5, 1984 an attempt to abduct Alhaji Umaru
Dikko – the erstwhile Minister of Transport and head of the Presidential
Task Force on Rice, and return him to Nigeria via a diplomatic crate
failed, thus leading to worsening relations between Nigeria and Britain.

Nigeria's relations with immediate neighboring states in West and
Central Africa were badly affected by the regime's domestic economic
revival policies and programs. These include prolonged border closure
partly meant to prevent politicians from fleeing the country with their
loot, expulsion of illegal aliens, and currency change, which adversely
affected the internal political economy of the neighboring states.

Part of the Buhari regime's ten-point programme outlined in a
world press conference shortly after taking power was 'eradication of
corruption.' The regime promulgated a number of rather draconian
decrees intended to curb corruption and other practices deemed
injurious to the health of the economy, including Decree Nos. 20, 21,
and 22 of 1984. These decrees prescribed harsh penalties, including
death by firing squad, for a variety of economic crimes such as illegal
oil bunkering, tampering with the free flow of petroleum products,
tampering with electricity and NEPA installations, cocaine addiction
and drug trafficking, currency counterfeiting and trafficking etc.

By October 1984, various tribunals set up under the Recovery of Public Property (Special Military Tribunals) Decree of 1984 had recouped amounts in excess of N112 million and £688,000 from politicians, over N348 million from FEDECO, and about N48.5 million from the National Assembly. The quest for repatriation of Nigeria's looted funds was further dampened by the British government's threat to publish the names and account details of all Nigerians with bank accounts in the United Kingdom.

Importantly, the Buhari regime's "War against Indiscipline" was meant to instill the ideals of national consciousness, patriotism and discipline in the citizenry. However, the regime's anti-corruption drive came under severe criticisms for among others, its selective nature and the secrecy surrounding corruption trials, the undermining of basic rules of evidence, discriminatory pattern of confirmation or revision of sentences, and double standards in government's implementation of tribunal verdicts (Osaghae: 1998).

The Buhari/Idiagbon regime known for its draconian policies at home and hardline postures abroad, was responsible for the contempt with which Nigeria was treated in the West African region, as well as the disdain the British had for the country during the period.

3.3.4 General Ibrahim Babangida (1985 – 1993)

General Babangida came to power in a military coup on August 27, 1985. The major pre-occupations of Babangida's foreign policy were outlined in his maiden speech of August 28, 1985 and include the following:

- Africa should remain the cornerstone of Nigeria's foreign policy.
- Realization of the objectives of the Organization of African Unity
- Rebirth of the Economic Community of West African States
- Continued membership of the United Nations Organization and other IGOs
- The call for a new International Economic Order
- Non-Aligned Movement
- Resolving Nigeria's debt plight

The All-Nigeria Conference on Foreign Policy convened by the Babangida regime in April 1986 at Kuru, Jos recommended an activist foreign policy thrust that is predicated on a strong, self-reliant, modern economy and a formidable military-industrial complex. A sound, independent economy, according to the Conference, is necessary for the pursuit of a non-aligned policy as well as the security and defense of the country (Akinterinwa: 2007).

General Babangida made significant impact at the continental level with his election as the OAU chairman. He presided over the signing of the treaty establishing the African Economic Community (EEC), and mediated in many intra African conflicts including Mali and Burkina Faso, the Chadian conflict, Senegal and Mauritania, the Sudan conflict, as well as the ECOMOG intervention in Liberia. Nigeria under General Babangida participated in several UN peace-keeping missions such as in Namibia, Rwanda, Somalia and Yugoslavia.

Other milestones of the Babangida foreign policy include Nigeria's decision to join the Organization of Islamic Conference (OIC) in 1986, the restoration of diplomatic relations with Israel, and the official pursuit of reparation (Nwosu: 2007).

In order to address economic downturn experienced in Nigeria from the early 1980s, characterized by fall in oil prices, rise in interest rates, collapse in commodity prices, and unsustainable debt profile, the Babangida regime instituted a Structural Adjustment Program (SAP) in line with IMF recommendations and devalued the Naira through the instrumentality of the Second-Tier Foreign Exchange Market (SFEM). SAP according to Asobie (1990: 20), is

> ... a diplomacy directed primarily at maximizing the inflow of foreign investment, enhancing the prospects of promoting Nigeria's export and facilitating the rescheduling of Nigeria's external debts.

General Babangida adopted economic diplomacy as the main thrust of his regime's foreign policy, defined by his erstwhile Minister of Foreign Affairs – General Ike Nwachukwu, as the task of using foreign policy "to achieve Nigeria's economic development and economic goals."

The major thrust and achievements of Nigeria's economic diplomacy during the Babangida era include –

1. Creation of awareness of the role of the organized private sector (OPS) in the nation's export drive through participation in various government-sponsored trade missions, Joint Commission meetings, and investment forums.
2. Restoration of Nigeria's credit worthiness, as evidenced by fresh credit grants in aid to support the SAP.
3. Halt to divestment and modest increase in foreign direct investment into the country with an aggregate value in 1985 (N6 million), 1986 (N9.31 million), and in 1987 (N9.99 million).
4. Improved trade relations in the area of non-oil export resulting to increased earnings in 1987 (N1.3 billion), 1988 (N2.757 billion), 1989 (N2.954 billion) and in 1991 (N4.07 billion).

However, the gains of Babangida's economic diplomacy has been disputed by Humphrey Asobie, as not serving Nigeria's national interest and not accelerating the rate of net capital inflow to Nigeria. Osaghae (1998) notes that foreign investment remained sluggish and was mostly directed towards the oil sector, while disinvestment plagued the industrial and manufacturing sectors during the Babangida regime. Over 150 multinational corporations (MNCs) divested from Nigeria since 1995, while more than 60 per cent of local industries, mostly small scale enterprises folded up since 1986, when SAP was introduced.

Similarly, the late Professor Olajide Aluko disagreed with the government's interpretation of Nigeria's economic problem, arguing that the country's problem is "gross mismanagement of resources, misallocation of resources and incompetence in public life and not attracting foreign investment." Another major constraint of Babangida's economic policy was the perpetuation of fraud in private sector business transactions;

> ...the issues of bad, sometimes fraudulent business practices by Nigerian exporters and businessmen, a phenomenon which has earned notoriety as 419 with

consequent deleterious effect on the credibility of Nigerian operators within the international business community (Akinsanya et al: 1991: 132).

Business scams of varying magnitudes by government collaborators also thrived during this period. In fact, the military administration's lack of accountability is said to have provided the foundation on which the 419 scam was built (Abegunrin: 2003).

In January 1986, Babangida set up a 17-member body (Political Bureau) chaired by Justice Samuel Cookey to conduct a national debate on the political future of Nigeria, "as the launching pad for the new Nigeria: prosperous, humanist and stable at home. A nation that possesses real capability in the African context and that commands and compels respect in international affairs." In its final report, the Bureau warned that;

> Corruption and indiscipline are two of the most serious problems which have confronted the Nigerian political process since independence. These twin problems reached scandalous dimensions during the last civilian regime. Nigerians are indeed unanimous in believing that any effort at erecting a new political order which does not tackle these twin problems of corruption and indiscipline is bound to fail (Cookey: 1987: 212).

In spite of this early warning, it is on record that General Babangida presided over one of the most corrupt regimes in Nigeria, characterized by a patron-client relationship, or what some have described as the politics of settlement whereby the regime perpetuates its authority through large-scale patronage networks involving both the ruling elite as well as the most vocal elements in civil society.

Testimonies at the Justice Oputa Panel revealed the regular sharing of crude oil or petroleum licenses among members of the Armed Forces Ruling Council (AFRC), as well as their collaboration in the bunkering and smuggling of petroleum products (Abegunrin: 2003).

The Pius Okigbo Panel on the Reform of the Central Bank of Nigeria set up by the succeeding Abacha regime, revealed the frittering away of almost $12.4 billion oil revenue windfall from the Gulf War by the Babangida administration under the so-called "dedicated and special" accounts. The Panel reported, among others;

- $12.2 billion was liquidated in less than six years
- They were spent on what could neither be adjudged genuine high priority nor truly regenerative investment
- Neither the president not the governor accounted to anyone for these massive extra-budgetary expenditures
- These disbursement were clandestinely undertaken while the country was openly reeling with a crushing external debt overhang

The Panel concluded that the creation of the "dedicated and special" account amounted to gross abuse of public trust, and recommended the immediate closure of the account and transfer of the outstanding balance of $206 million to Nigeria's external reserve (Oko-Osi: 2007).

Other cases of corruption during General Babangida's regime involved government parastatals such as the Customs, Inland Revenue Department, National Youth Service Corp, National Electric Power Authority, Nigerian Airways, Nigerian Telecommunications Limited, Nigerian National Petroleum Company, the Nigerian Police Force, etc. Public buildings were often set ablaze in an effort to destroy evidence of fraud and corrupt practices (Agedah: 1993).

According to Osaghae (1998: 189);

> The Babangida years were (also) some of the country's worst years, with unprecedented levels of bureaucratic corruption, repression and political turbulence. New dimensions of political instability such as letter-bombs, assassinations and aircraft hijacking were added to the list.

The Babangida administration enjoyed the support and approval of the international community, notably Britain, France and the United

States, while its transition program appeared to be on course. Upon cancellation of the June 12 1993 presidential election purportedly won by Chief M. K. O. Abiola and adjudged as the freest and fairest election in the nation's electoral history, the Babangida regime quickly lost its domestic political support and attracted international sanctions.

Both Osaghae (1998) and Saliu (1999) agree that the annulment of the June 12 presidential election was the greatest catalyst of Nigeria's descent into anarchy, setting off, on the international scene, Nigeria's steady march towards becoming a so-called pariah state. Ironically, part of the reasons advanced by General Babangida for the annulment of the June 12 election was evidence according to the regime, of over N2.1 billion in monetary inducements paid by the presidential candidates to secure votes (Diamond et al: 1997). Another catalyst for Nigeria's declining international image during the Babangida era was the country's emerging profile as a major channel in the world drug trade, leading among others, to the decertification of the country by the United States, which in turn resulted to blocking of aid and placement of embargo on direct flights between the United States and Nigeria.

Beginning from 1985, a hostile external environment intensively dominated by the worldwide economic recession of the 1980s, the consequent adverse effects on Nigeria's foreign exchange earnings, rampant internal corruption, and excessive personalization of decision making combined to weaken the thrust and effectiveness of Nigerian foreign policy (Abegunrin: 2003).

3.3.5 General Sani Abacha (1993 – 1998)

General Sani Abacha took over government from the Interim National Government (ING) headed by Chief Ernest Shonekan in a palace coup on November 17, 1993. The ING to which the Babangida regime handed over power, had embarked on an anti-corruption crusade involving the dissolution of the boards of NNPC and its subsidiaries, and putting NNPC's Managing Director – Edmund Dakoru and other top officials of the corporation on trial, as well as sending an anti-corruption bill to the National Assembly.

General Abacha did not articulate a clear foreign policy during his tenure, rather, series of his tragic domestic policies snowballed into diplomatic controversies, including his crackdown on pro-democracy activists, gross abuse of human rights and fundamental freedoms, the arrest and detention of Chief Abiola in June 1994, the March 1995 phantom coup, the November 1995 hanging of Ken Saro-Wiwa and eight Ogoni activists, and the controversial coup plot of December 1997. Fawole (1999: 19) outlines the defining parameters of Abacha's foreign policy in terms of;

> The arrest and detention of Chief Moshood Abiola in June, 1994; the coup hoax of March 1995 in which several military officers and prominent opponents of the junta, including former head of state Olusegun Obasanjo and his deputy, Major-General Shehu Musa Yar'adua, were framed up and convicted; and the hanging of Ken Saro-Wiwa and eight Ogoni leaders after a flawed trial in November 1995.

The only exception was perhaps Nigeria's participation in the ECOMOG operations in Liberia, which received $10 million in assistance from the U. S. government in October 1996. Otherwise, Abacha's domestic politics constituted a huge liability on Nigeria's foreign policy.

General Abacha embarked on a corrective anti-corruption crusade including the setting up of panels to probe corrupt government departments and agencies, notably Nigerian Custom Service (NCS); Nigerian Ports Authority (NPA); Central Bank of Nigeria (CBN); Nigerian Airports Authority (NPA); NITEL; and NNPC. Of particular significance was the Pius Okigbo-panel on the CBN which uncovered the frittering away of almost $12.4 billion windfall oil revenues from the Gulf War by the Babangida administration under the so-called "dedicated and special" accounts.

Perhaps the most effective anti-corruption measure of the Abacha regime was the promulgation of the Failed Banks and Other Financial Institutions (BOFI) Decree of 1994 setting up tribunals to prosecute bank officials and their customers whose reckless acts had led to the collapse of many commercial merchant banks at the time. Abacha (1993) had indicated in his coup speech that "Drug trafficking and other economic crimes such as 419 must be tackled and eliminated." To these ends, the National Drug Law Enforcement Agency (NDLEA) was set up, and the Advance Fee Fraud and other Related Offences Decree of 1995 was signed into law on April 1, 1995.

Notwithstanding, it is on record that General Abacha and some of his ministers, family members, security chiefs and business friends participated in large scale looting of the national treasury. The exact amount that Abacha stole from the state is unknown, but is thought to be in excess of $3 billion. Transparency International ranked Abacha among the top 5 political looters of all time (Table 3.2)

Table 3.2 Estimate of Stolen Assets by 5 Political Leaders

	Political Leader	Country	Stolen Assets ($bn)
1.	Mohamed Suharto (1967 – 98)	Indonesia	15 to 35
2.	Ferdinand Marcos (1972 – 86)	Philippines	5 to 10
3.	Mobutu Sese Seko (1965 – 97)	Zaire	5
4.	Sanni Abacha (1993 – 98)	Nigeria	2 to 5
5.	Slobodan Milosevic (1989 – 2000)	Serbia/ Yugoslavia	1

Source: TI (2004) quoted in UNODC (2007)

In collaboration with his associates, Abacha purchased for $500 million the $2.5 billion debt that Nigerian owed to Russia for the Ajaokuta steelworks, and paid himself the full sum from the national treasury. He also pillaged the oil industry, including $190 million that Elf Aquitaine admitted to paying him. By May 2009, some $1.9 billion had been recovered from the late Abacha, and the whereabouts of another $700 million was also established (Iliffe: 2011).

Chief Dan Etete – Abacha's Minister of Petroleum Resources was reported to have been duped of $200 million in October 1996, and in November 2007, a French court sentenced Chief Etete to three years in prison and a fine of €250 million for money laundering. Chief Etete was convicted of using €15 million in funds obtained fraudulently to purchase luxury properties in 1999 and 2000 in France. Abacha himself reportedly acquired over $6 billion with properties and investments worth CFA500 million in Britain alone (Okeke: 2004).

Foreign investors continued to shun Nigeria in spite of the repeal of two anti-FDI laws – the Exchange Control Act of 1962 and the Enterprises Promotion Decree of 1972 by the Abacha regime. Capital flight and divestment by foreign companies was the norm. MNCs that reduced their holdings in Nigeria between 1993 and 1994 include Standard Chartered bank, the Wellcome Foundation, and Unilever Plc (Osaghae: 1998). Reasons for the foreign divestment include Nigeria's political crises, the bad reputation of Nigerians abroad and the refusal of the Bretton-Woods institutions to endorse the Abacha regime's economic policies (Okeke: 2004).

In response to the regime's execution of Ken Saro-Wiwa and his fellow activists on November 10, 1995, the Commonwealth suspended Nigeria's membership for two years. The United Nations also sent a fact-finding team, whose report seriously indicted the regime for gross human rights abuses. Many other countries reacted to the executions through the recall of ambassadors, imposition of visa restrictions on military personnel and government officials, sports boycott by the European Union, etc.

Under General Abacha's regime and his abusive foreign policy, which Ambassador Gabriel Olusanya – the former Director General of the Nigerian Institute of International Affairs (NIIA) branded "Area Boy Diplomacy," Nigeria further descended into pariah status and the country's image took a turn for the worse. In the wake of broadening international isolation of Nigeria, which had its roots from the annulment of the June 12 election, Abacha explained that;

> We have, in recent times, been looking beyond our traditional allies, to diversify and cultivate new ties with countries that we consider not only friendly but display honest desire to cooperate with us in the pursuit of our development objectives (Oche: 1999).

The Abacha regime sought for new friends among the ranks of fellow pariahs like Colonel Muammar Ghadaffi of Libya, General Omar el-Bashir of the Sudan, Yahya Jammeh of Gambia, and Mainassara Barre of Nigeria Republic. It also dispatched high profile emissaries to Iran, Iraq, Indonesia, North Korea, and China.

The Washington Post reports that the Abacha regime spent over $10 million in lobbying and public relations campaigns since the hanging of the Ogoni activists. Among his foremost lobbyists were Senator Carol Mosley-Braun; Reverend Henry J. Lyons; Roy Innis; and Louis Farrakhan. Yet, as Abegunrin (2003: 154) surmises;

> ... under Abacha, Nigeria became a haven for drug dealers, which together with other criminal activities by individuals abroad, such as 419 frauds, and the hanging of Ken Saro-Wiwa and his fellow Ogoni activists, made Nigeria a pariah in the eyes of the international community.

The isolation of Nigeria by the international community during the Abacha regime extended to the field of sports and specifically soccer, when FIFA – the world soccer governing body, cancelled the 8th World Youth Football Championship scheduled for Nigeria in 1995 on grounds of political instability and security concerns (Fawole: 1999). The Catholic Pontiff – Pope John Paul also joined in calling on General Abacha to end corruption and repressive rule, and demonstrate respect for human rights, during his visit to Nigeria in March 1998.

However, the sudden death of General Sani Abacha on June 8, 1998 presented Nigeria with fresh opportunities to embark on a new mission to resolve its political crisis, revive its economy, and add fillip to its foreign policy.

3.3.6 General Abdulsalami Abubakar (1998 – 1999)

General Abdulsalami Abubakar assumed power on June 8, 1998 following the sudden death of General Abacha and immediately began the process of reversing the obnoxious policies of his predecessor in office. General Abubakar repealed many of Abacha's draconian decrees and released over 140 political prisoners and union leaders. Discussions were ongoing to release Chief M. K. O. Abiola when he died suddenly on July 7, 1998. General Abubakar publicly declared that he had no political ambition and rolled out a political transition program that would usher in a civilian democratic government within a year.

In his July 20 address, General Abubakar promised that his interim military government would be committed to improving the country's external image, and would actively participate in the promotion of global peace, stability and progress. His regime gained credibility from the visit of eminent international personalities including the UN Secretary General Kofi Anan, Commonwealth Secretary General Emeka Anyaoku as well as high level British and American delegations. General Abubakar was also allowed to travel to world capitals including Paris, London and Washington, to confer with his counterparts. He also attended the summit of the Non-Aligned Movement in Durban, South Africa.

Within his one year of leadership of Nigeria, General Abubakar was able to restore some semblance of honour and integrity to the country and ended its international isolation because of his sincere desire to relinquish power at the expiration of his regime's short transition programme.

Anti-corruption measures announced by the Abubakar regime include open competitive tendering for government contracts, elimination of the dual exchange rate, a more transparent system for the importation of petroleum products, as well as a requirement that all senior military officials of government declare their assets (IfeomaChuku: 2004). General Abubakar also set in motion the process of recovering millions of dollars looted by the Abacha regime, including $500 million stashed away by Ismail Gwarzo – the erstwhile National Security Adviser (NSA).

Notwithstanding, the regime of General Abdulsalami Abubakar depleted the national treasury in unbudgeted and unaccounted for government expenditures. The country's foreign reserve was depleted from $7.1 billion in January 1999 to $3.75 billion as of May 1999. As if this was not enough, General Abubakar also signed into law a generous retirement package for Nigeria's heads of state and their deputies just before leaving office.

The Christopher Kolade panel set up by the succeeding President Obasanjo recommended the cancellation of 1,684 of 4,072 contracts, 755 out of 768 national awards, 19 of 576 licenses, 107 of 111 approvals, and 50 of 807 appointments made under General Abubakar's regime, for violations of the basic principles of planning accountability and transparency. The Panel observed a public service characterized by lack of standards and indiscipline, adding that most of the expenditures on projects during the period were extra-budgetary and the bulk of projects in rolling plans were not always the ones eventually executed in annual budgets (Ilife: 2011).

Jude Uddoh, Ph.D.

References
Chapter Three

Abacha, Sani (1993) Coup Speech of November 17, 1993
http://www.citizensfornigeria.com/library/
speeches/1211-coup-speech-of-general-sani-abacha-november-17-1993

Abegunrin, Olayiwola (2003) *Nigerian Foreign Policy under Military Rule, 1966-1999* Westport, Praeger Publishers

Adeniran, Tunde (1985) "The Terrain and Tenor of Nigeria's Foreign Policy" in Atanda J. A. and Aliyu, A. Y. (Eds) (1985) *Proceedings of the National Conference on Nigeria since Independence. Volume : Political Development.* Zaria, The Panel on Nigeria Since Independence History Project. Pp. 188 – 201.

Akinsanya, Olusegun et al (1991) *Nigeria's Economic Diplomacy (The Ike Nwachukwu Years, 1988 – 1992)* Nigeria, Ministry of Foreign Affairs

Akinterinwa, Bola A. (2007) *General Ibrahim Babangida's Legacy: Domestic and International Dimensions* Malthouse Monographs on Africa No. 5. Lagos, Malthouse Press Limited. Pp. 47 – 82.

Asobie, Asisi H. (1990) "Nigeria: Economic Diplomacy and National Interest. An Analysis of the Policies of Nigeria's External economic Relations, with Special Reference to Ibrahim Babangida's Administration. Paper presented at the 16th Annual Conference of the Nigerian Society of International Affairs. Lagos, NIIA Nov. 5 – 6, 1990. P. 20

Chuku, Gloria I. (2004) "Quest for National Purification: Murtala Mohammed's New Vision, 1975-1976" in Nwachuku, Levi A. and Uzoigwe, G. N. (2004) *Trouble Journey: Nigeria Since the Civil War* Dallas, University Press of America Inc.

Cookey, Samuel J. (1987) *Report of the Political Bureau* Lagos, Federal Government Printer

Diamond Larry, Kirk-Green Anthony, and Oyediran Oyeleye (Eds) (1997) *Transition Without End: Nigerian Politics and Civil Society under Babangida* London, Lynne Rienner Publishers

Falola, Toyin (1998) "Corruption in the Nigerian Public Service: 1945 – 1960" in Mbaku, John M. (1998) *Corruption and the Crisis of Institutional Reforms in Africa* Lewiston, Edwin Mellen Press. Pp. 137-163

Fawole, Alade W (2003) *Nigeria's External Relations and Foreign Policy under Military Rule, 1966 – 1999* Ile-Ife, Obafemi Awolowo University Press Ltd.

Fawole, Alade W. (1999) *Paranoia, Hostility and Defiance: General Sani Abacha and the "New" Nigerian Foreign Policy* Ile-Ife, Obafemi Awolowo University Press

Iliffe, John (2011) *Obasanjo, Nigeria and the World* Suffolk, James Currey

Metz, Helen C. (Ed) (1991) *Nigeria: A Country Study.* Washington, Library of Congress

Njoku, O. N. (2004) "Era of Misguided Good Feelings: Yakubu Gowon and the Birth of a New Nigeria, 1970-1975," in Nwachuku, Levi A. and Uzoigwe, G. N. (2004) *Trouble Journey: Nigeria Since the Civil War* Dallas, University Press of America Inc.

Nwachuku, Levi A. (2004) "Crisis of Purpose: General Muhmamadu Buhari's Renaissance of National Sanitation, 1984-1985" in Nwachuku, Levi A. and Uzoigwe, G. N. (2004) *Trouble Journey: Nigeria Since the Civil War* Dallas, University Press of America Inc.

Nwachuku, Levi A. (2004) "Vision Betrayed? Olusegun Obasanjo, 1976-1979" in Nwachuku, Levi A. and Uzoigwe, G. N. (2004) *Trouble Journey: Nigeria Since the Civil War* Dallas, University Press of America Inc.

Nwosu, Nereus I (2007) *Nigeria's Foreign Policy under General Babangida* Malthouse Monographs on Africa. Nos. 6. Lagos, Malthouse Press Limited. Pp. 89 – 116.

Nzeogwu, Chukwuma K. (1966) *Radio Broadcast Announcing Nigeria's First Military Coup on Radio Nigeria, Kaduna* Vanguard September 30, 2010

Oche, Ogaba (1999) "Nigeria's Policy Shift to Asia" in Saliu, Hassan A. (Ed.) (1999) *Selected Themes in Nigerian Foreign Policy & International Relations* Ilorin, Sally and Associates pp. 62 – 74, at 69

Okeke, Okechukwu (2004) "Legacy of National Paralysis: Ernest Shonekan and Sani Abacha, 1993-1998 in Nwachuku, Levi A. and Uzoigwe, G. N. (2004) *Trouble Journey: Nigeria Since the Civil War* Dallas, University Press of America Inc.

Oko-Osi, Antonia T. (2007) *Corruption and Corrupt Practices: Institutionalization and Legitimization under the Babangida Administration* Malthouse Monographs on Africa No. 7. Lagos, Malthouse Press Limited pp. 8 – 33.

Osaghae, Eghosa E. (1998) *Crippled Giant: Nigeria since Independence* Bloomington, Indiana University Press

Saliu, Hassan A. (1999) "Limitations of Nigerian Foreign Policy" in Aliu, Hasan A (Ed) (1999) *Selected Themes in Nigerian Foreign Policy and International relations* Ilorin, Sally and Associates pp. 121 – 140

Uzoigwe, G. N. and Effah-Attoe, Stella A. (2004) "Vision Lost: Restoration of Civilian Rule and Shehu Shagari's Missed Opportunity, 1979-1983" in Nwachuku, Levi A. and Uzoigwe, G. N. (2004) *Trouble Journey: Nigeria Since the Civil War* Dallas, University Press of America Inc.

Chapter Four

CORRUPTION AND NIGERIAN FOREIGN POLICY UNDER THE ADMINISTRATION OF PRESIDENT OLUSEGUN OBASANJO

> Corruption in Nigeria constrains the country's economic development and consequently its economic and political reach regionally and internationally (Nuamah: 2003: 4).

> The impact of official corruption is so rampant and has earned Nigeria a very bad image at home and abroad (Obasanjo: 1999).

Introduction

In this Chapter, we will consider three broad typologies of corruption during the Obasanjo administration, as well as the impact of corruption on Nigerian foreign policy.

4.1.0 Broad Typologies of Corruption during the Obasanjo Administration

Three broad typologies of corruption discussed in this section are public sector corruption; private sector corruption; and electoral corruption.

4.1.1 Public Sector Corruption

Grand/Political Corruption:

Grand corruption, also known as political corruption takes place at the highest levels of political authority. It usually involves heads of states, ministers and top officials, who exploit their positions to extract large bribes from national and transnational corporations. They appropriate significant pay-offs from contract scams and embezzle large sums of money from the public treasury into private, often overseas bank accounts (Andvig and Fjeldstad: 2000). Some cases of grand/political corruption during the administration of President Olusegun Obasanjo include the following:

Tafa Balogun – Inspector General of Police:

Inspector General of Police – Tafa Balogun was convicted on a guilty plea involving an 8-count charge of money laundering, and sentenced to 6 months imprisonment and forfeiture of assets totaling $150 million including money stashed in banks, shares in blue chip companies and 14 luxury buildings. Balogun was said to have incorporated companies to loot the police treasury through bribes and kickbacks on contracts. Billions of naira were fraudulently withdrawn by him from the police account and transferred to the companies to buy blue chip shares, landed properties, and foreign currency (Transparency for Nigeria: 2003).

Diepriye Alamieyesegha – Governor of Bayelsa State:

Alamieyesegha was convicted in July 2007 on guilty plea to a 6-count charge of false declaration of assets and a 23-count charge of money laundering by his companies, and was sentenced to 2 years imprisonment. His conviction paved the way for recovery of over $17.7 million in stolen assets, and a world-wide freeze in assets variously located in the United Kingdom, South Africa, Nigeria, Denmark, and Cyprus. The Metropolitan Police in London first arrested Alamieyesegha at Heathrow airport in September 2005 on suspicion of money laundering. An investigation revealed that Alamieyesegha had about $1.5 million cash stuffed in suitcases in his London home, funds in bank accounts amounting to $2.7 million, as well as London real estate worth an estimated $15 million. The US Department of Justice subsequently froze $400,000 brokerage fund and a $600,000 Maryland home traced to Alamieyesegha (Edwards et al: 2008).

Olabode George – Deputy National Chairman PDP and Chairman Nigerian Ports Authority:

Olabode George and five others were on October 2009 convicted on 35 out of a 68-count charge bordering on about N100 billion contract splitting, inflation, abuse of office and disobedience to lawful order, and sentenced to 2-year imprisonment without option of fine. They were said to have inflated the price of contract awarded to Kalmer West Africa Limited from €215,555.52 (being the prevailing price at the time of the award of the contract) to €269,965.71. Olabode George was initially cleared of allegations of impropriety in the management of the Board of Nigerian Ports Authority, brought against him by the EFCC under President Olusegun Obasanjo. George completed his sentencing and was welcomed out of prison by thousands of party supporters and senior government officials (Abdulah: 2009).

James Ibori – Governor of Delta State:

James Ibori was convicted by the Southwark Crown Court London in February 2012 and sentenced to 13 years in prison based on his admission of a 10-count charge of conspiracy to defraud and money laundering estimated at $250 million. Among Ibori's assets that were confiscated, are;

- A house in Hampstead, North London worth £2.2 million
- A property in Shaftesbury, Dorset valued at £311,000
- A mansion in Sandton, South Africa worth £3.2 million
- A fleet of armored Range Rovers valued at £600,000
- A Bentley Continental GT valued at £120,000
- A Mercedes Benz Maybach 62 bought for €407,000

Ibori was arrested in the United Arab Emirate by INTERPOL based on an international arrest warrant by the British government on money laundering charges and extradited to the United Kingdom where he was subsequently arraigned.

London Metropolitan Police had secured an order from a London court in 2007 to freeze $35 million worth of Ibori's foreign assets including a private jet. On December 17, 2009 a High Court sitting in Asaba Delta State discharged and acquitted Ibori of a 170-count charge involving money laundering. In June 2010, Ibori's Sister Christine Ibie-Ibori and acquaintance Udoamaka Okonkwo were found guilty of money laundering charges and were each sentenced to 5 years imprisonment by the Southwark Crown Court. His lawyer Bhadresh Gohil was sentenced to 10 years. Ibori was previously convicted in 1991 for stealing from Wickes DIY store in Naesden, North-West London, where he worked as a cashier (Ajaero: 2012).

Bribery of Public Officials by Multinational Corporations (MNCs)

Foreign multinational corporations (MNCs) provide what is commonly referred to as "the supply side" of corruption, by bribing local politicians and public officials in order to secure lucrative contracts. President Obasanjo acknowledged in his inaugural speech that, "… grand corruption has always involved (Nigeria's) foreign trading friends as well."

Transparency International publishes the Bribe Payers Index (BPI) which ranks the leading exporting countries in terms of the degree to which their companies are perceived to be paying bribes to win or retain business abroad (Table 4.1).

Table 4.1 Bribe Payers Index (1999, 2002 and 2006)

	1999	2002	2006
1.	China	China	India
2.	South Korea	Taiwan	China
3.	Taiwan	South Korea	Russia
4.	Italy	Italy	Turkey
5.	Malaysia	Hong Kong	Taiwan

| 6. | Japan | Malaysia | Malaysia |
| 7. | Singapore | France | Saudi Arabia |

Source: Transparency International <u>www.transparency.org</u>

In 1999 and 2002, China took the lead among countries whose MNCs were perceived to be paying bribes to obtain businesses abroad followed by South Korea and Taiwan respectively. In 2006, India took the lead followed by China and Russia. On the average, Chinese MNCs were perceived to be most involved in bribing foreign officials for the respective periods of 1999, 2002 and 2006. USA was ranked 10th position in 1999 and 8th position in 2002. France was ranked 7th position in 1999 and 9th position in 2002, while Russia was ranked 3rd position in 2006.

Several US-affiliated companies have been penalized for bribing Nigerian public officials in breach of the U.S. Foreign Corrupt Practices Act (FCPA) 1978 (Table 4.2).

Table 4.2 U.S. FCPA Enforcement Action Concerning Nigeria

	Company	Offence (Period)	Penalty ($ mn)*
1.	Panalpina, Inc.	Bribery of Custom Officials (2002-2007)	70.56
2.	Tidewater, Inc.	Bribery of Custom Officials (2002-2007)	7.35
3.	GlobalSantaFe Corp.	Bribery of Custom Officials (2002-2007)	2.1
4.	Noble Corporation	Bribery of Custom Officials (2003-2007)	2.59
5.	Royal Dutch Shell Plc.	Bribery of Custom Officials (2002-2005)	30
6.	ENI/Snamprogetti	Bribery of Govt. Officials (2002-2003)	365
7.	Technip	Bribery of Govt. Officials (1995-2004)	240
8.	Daimler AG	Bribery of Govt. Officials	93.6
9.	KBR/Haliburton	Bribery of Govt. Officials(1994-2002)	402
10.	Wilbros	Bribery of Govt. Officials (From 2003)	10.3
11.	Baker Hughes	Bribery of Custom Officials (2001-2005)	10

| 12. | J.B. Brown (Wilbros) | Bribery of Govt. Officials (From 2005) | Ongoing |
| 13. | ABB Ltd | Bribery of Govt. Officials (1998-2003) | 10 |

Source: U.S. Security and Exchange Commission
*Penalty does not include injunction and disgorgement fees.

Panalpina Inc., Tidewaters Inc., GlobalSantaFe Corp., Noble Corp., and Royal Dutch Shell Plc were at different times indicted by the U.S. Securities and Exchange Commission for bribing Nigerian Customs Services (NCS) officials for flouting various aspects of the import/export regulations or for obtaining preferential treatment in the customs process pertaining to their personnel and equipment.

Snamprogetti and other joint venture companies authorized the hiring of two agents, a U.K. solicitor and a Japanese trading company, through which more than $180 million in bribes were funneled to Nigerian government officials to obtain several contracts to build liquefied natural gas (LNG) facilities on Bonny Island, Nigeria. Technip and other members of TSKJ, a four-company joint venture that includes KBR, Inc., bribed Nigerian government officials to win contracts to build a $6 billion liquefied natural gas (LNG) production facility in Nigeria.

Over a 10-year period, KBR subsidiary Kellogg Brown & Root LLC through agents paid $180 million bribe to accounts controlled by Nigerian government officials and beginning in 2002 paid $5 million in cash to a Nigerian political party to obtain construction contracts worth more than $6 billion.

From 2003, Willbros Group paid more than $6 million bribes to Nigerian government officials and employees of an operator of a joint venture majority-owned by the Nigerian government in order to obtain two major contracts with net profits of almost $9 million. Brown, a former supervisory employee in Wilbros's Nigerian and Latin American operations was accused of procuring and delivering bribe payments of $1 million and another of $550,000 to Nigerian government officials and to employees of the operator of a joint venture majority owned by an arm of the Nigerian government in February and March of 2005.

Finally, ABB's U.S. and foreign-based subsidiaries doing business in Nigeria, Angola and Kazakhstan, offered and made illicit payments totaling over $1.1 million to government officials in these countries to obtain and retain business.

Petty Corruption

Petty or bureaucratic corruption takes place among lower level public officials and involves extortion of modest amounts of bribe from the public for routine administrative services such as hospitals, schools, local licensing authorities, police, custom, revenue authorities, etc. The extent of petty corruption in Nigeria is best illustrated by the Nigerian Governance and Corruption Survey Study, which aims among others, "To help identify government agencies with significant (corruption) problems that can be targeted for reform (Ministry of Finance: 2003)." The study is based on a nationally representative drawn from households, business enterprises and public officials.

Table 4.3 Ten Least Honest Public Institutions in Nigeria

S/N	Public Institution
1.	Police
2.	Federal/State/LG Executive Council
3.	Political Party
4.	NEPA
5.	Members of National and State Assemblies
6.	Municipal/Local Government
7.	Courts
8.	Internal Revenue Board
9.	The Armed Forces/Military
10.	Custom Authority

Source: Ministry of Finance (2003)

Federal Ministries ranked in the study include Health; Education; Commerce; Works and Transport; and Agriculture and Natural Resources. The study indicates that petty/bureaucratic corruption is pervasive among public institutions in Nigeria. It ranked the Police as the least honest public institution in the country, followed by Federal/State/LG Executive Council, and Political party (Table 4.3). Other key findings of the study include the following:

- Households see corruption as a serious problem which is getting worse.
- Enterprises hold a very low opinion of the integrity of public institutions.
- Seven out of ten public officials believe corruption is pervasive, although modest and declining in their organizations.

The Obasanjo administration was accused of not doing enough to check low-level corruption, which was common at state and local government levels; "policemen pocketing bribes at roadblocks, teachers demanding settlement before granting school places, or nurses extorting payment from their patients.' As the regime's inability to tackle corruption became clear, so its public approval rating in this area fell between 2000 and 2003 from 64% to 24% (Ilife: 2011).

4.1.2 Private Sector Corruption

The local parlance for advance fee fraud (AFF) is "419" derived from Chapter 38 of the Nigerian Criminal Code which provides for the offence of obtaining by false pretense, cheating. Section 419 provides inter alia:

> Any person who by false pretense, and with intent to defraud, obtains from any other person anything capable of being stolen, or induces any other person to deliver to any person anything capable of being stolen, is guilty of a felony, and is liable to imprisonment for three years.

The definition and punishment for this offence have been modified under the Advance Fee Fraud and other Related Offences Decree of 1995 which was signed into law by General Sani Abacha on April 1, 1995. The Decree extends the application of the offence to include acts committed outside Nigeria as well as its punishment upon conviction to a term of not more than 20 years and not less than seven years without an option of fine.

The US Department of State (1997) has chronicled some of the most common forms of AFF practiced by Nigerians as including transfer of money for over-invoiced contracts, contract fraud (C.O.D. of goods and services), conversion of hard currency (black money), sale of crude oil below market prices, purchase of real estate, disbursement of money from wills, threat scam (extortion), and clearing house. Some reported cases of Nigerian involvement in AFF include the following:

Adedeji Alumile (a.k.a. Ade Bendel):

Mr. Alumile was found guilty of defrauding Abdel Azim Attia, an Egyptian General, of over $500,000 (N65 million) in 2003. After a protracted case at an Ikeja High Court, he was sentenced to six years imprisonment. Delivering judgment on the matter, Justice Mufutau Olokooba described his action as an international embarrassment to the nation.

Chief Fred Ajudua:

Mr. Ajudua is currently serving jail sentence for involvement in "419" charges. He obtained the sum of $285,000 from Nelson Allen, a Canadian through mail fraud. Mr. Allen came to Nigeria to give evidence of the transaction during the trial. Other victims of Mr. Ajudua include Technex Import and Export Company of Germany which lost $230,000, and Frieda Springer-Beck, also a German who lost $350,000. The trial process in Springer-Beck's case was adjourned 92 times and the victim observed that Mr. Ajudua was regularly escorted to court by armed police. The court heard evidence of how the German lady visited the Central Bank of Nigeria (CBN) with Mr. Ajudua and met an assistant director of the bank who "opened a file on his desk containing original documents of the contract and a check for $28.5 million" purportedly left by her late husband.

Honourable Maurice Ibekwe:

Hon. Maurice Ibekwe a member of the House of Representatives was prosecuted for defrauding a German citizen Munch Klause of $300,000 and DM75,000. Maurice Ibekwe was arraigned in court on July 29, 2003 and denied bail. He subsequently died in custody on March 20, 2004 (Ekeanyanwu et al: 2004)

Ikechukwu Christian Anajemba, Emmanuel Odinigwe Nwude, Nzeribe Okoli and Amaka Anajemba:

Between May 1995 and February 1998, Banco Noroeste S.A. of Brazil was defrauded of a total of $242 million through offshore banks in the Cayman Islands. Nelson Tetsuo Sakaguchi, a senior official of the bank transmitted the money by swift transfers to various bank accounts controlled by Ikechukwu Christian Anajemba, Emmanuel Odinigwe Nwude, Nzeribe Okoli and Amaka Anajemba on promises that he and other bank officials would receive a commission of $10 million.

The payments were made to secure the contract for construction of a purported second international Airport at Abuja. Criminal proceedings were instituted in a number of jurisdictions connected with the offence leading to the arrest, trial and conviction of the culprits. In Nigeria, the scammers were arraigned on an 86-count charge including;

> "...fraudulently obtaining through false pretence $242 million from one Nelson Sakaguchi and Stanton Development Corporation, being the property of Banco Noroeste S.A. of Sao Paulo, Brazil, purporting same to represent payment due for the construction of the Abuja International Airport."

They also fraudulently used false documents purporting them to emanate from the CBN, the Corporate Affairs Commission, the Presidency, and Federal Ministry of Aviation. Nwude and Okoli plead guilty to numerous crimes and forfeited $121.5 million in assets. Mr. Chris Anajemba died in the course of his trial while his wife also pleaded guilty and received a two and half year sentence after giving back $48.5 million.

Nigerians have particularly gained much notoriety for their involvement in AFF. At an Interpol meeting in 2003, 122 out of 138 countries represented complained about Nigerian involvement in financial fraud in their countries. Nigerian-style AFF is estimated to cost the British economy £150 million annually with the average losses per victim estimated at £31,000. Between 2000 and 2003, the National Criminal Intelligence Service (NCIS) identified 78,000 Nigerian-style letters, faxes and e-mails in London alone (Peel: 2006).

In their 2004 Annual Report, IC3 – an organization set up by the Federal Bureau of Investigation (FBI) and the National White Collar Crime Center to track the extent of fraud reported that 'Nigerian letter frauds' tended to be among the highest value crimes in terms of losses per victim. While the median loss to fraud was $219.56, the figure for 'Nigerian letter fraud' was $3,000. IC3 analysis of the nationalities of perpetrators of the frauds put Nigerians third behind only US and Canadian nationalities in terms of numbers. The FBI estimates financial fraud by Nigerian Criminal Enterprise at between one and two billion dollars in the United States alone (Peel: 2006).

Another organization - the US Internet Fraud Complaint Center (IFCC) calculates in its 2001 Internet Fraud Report that Nigerian letter fraud cases constitute about 15.5 per cent of all complaints. It also notes that "while the median loss in all manner of Internet fraud was US$435, in the Nigerian scams it was US$5,575". In its 2002 report, the organization noted that 74 people lost US$1.6 million in 16,000 complaints regarding Nigerian fraud communications (UNODC: 2005).

4.1.3 Electoral Corruption

Having won consecutive elections in 1999 and 2003, President Olesegun Obasanjo attempted to extend his term of office. A draft constitution with a proposal for an elongated term of office for the President and Governors was introduced to the National Political Reform Conference (NPRC). The proposal was endorsed by the Senator Ibrahim Mantu led Joint Constitutional Review Committee (JCRC) of the National

Assembly, but was subsequently turned down by the Senate in May 2006.

Having failed to secure another term, President Obasanjo sought not only to stop his Vice – Alhaji Atiku Abubakar from succeeding him but also to consolidate his position within the PDP by hand-picking his successor Governor of Katsina State - Umaru Yar'Adua, in an election that he described as a do-or-die affair (Nwabueze: 2007).

Elections for the 36 State Governors and 990 Legislators in the 36 State Houses of Assembly were held on 14 April 2007 and elections for the President of Nigeria, 109 Members of the Senate and 360 Members of the House of Representatives took place on 21 April 2007. The elections were conducted on the basis of the Electoral Act of 2006, which was criticized as leaving many unresolved issues around party finance and corruption.

The ruling Peoples Democratic Party's (PDP) won a majority in the 2007 general elections at all levels of government. The new government was inaugurated at national and state levels on 29 May 2007. However, the 2007 elections were reported by both domestic and international observers as having been riddled with a wide range of procedural "irregularities" and electoral frauds (Adetula: 2008).

Buhari's lawyers later claimed that only some 30,000 voters' names were ticked on the registers in Rivers State, where the PDP alone claimed some 2.7 million votes, the highest number in the country. In Anambra State, where there was little voting, Andy Uba was awarded 1.9 million votes by a registered electorate of 1.8 million. INEC later ordered fresh elections in 27 of the 36 states, but there were no prosecutions for electoral irregularities.

At the presidential level, whereas pre-election opinion polls suggested roughly equal votes for and against PDP, Yar'Adua won 70% of the reported votes, with 19% for Buhari and 8% for Atiku. The PDP also won a sweeping 90% of the seats in the National Assembly elections.

According to the Report of the European Union Election Observer Mission (EU EOM: 2007);

> The 2007 State and Federal elections fell far short of basic
> international and regional standards for democratic

elections. They were marred by very poor organization, lack of essential transparency, widespread procedural irregularities, substantial evidence of fraud, widespread voter disenfranchisement at different stages of the process, lack of equal conditions for political parties and candidates and numerous incidents of violence. As a result, the process cannot be considered to have been credible. Given the lack of transparency and evidence of fraud, particularly in the result collation process, there can be no confidence in the results of these elections.

Leaders of the European Parliament which endorsed the EU EOM statement added that two main features which emerged on both election days are "the inability of INEC to handle the process efficiently and the determination of Nigerians to cast their vote."

In the their own assessment of the 2007 general elections in Nigeria, the International Republican Institute (IRI: 2007) observed that;

The 2007 Nigerian elections were a failure both of will from the country's political leadership and of logistical preparation by INEC. The former preordained the outcome of the elections before voters went to the polls, while the latter's decisions prevented many Nigerians from voting.

Other key findings of the Institute include the following,

- The ruling PDP, under President Obasanjo, used the EFCC to eliminate and intimidate opponents, including those within the PDP.
- Public officials' immunity from prosecution motivated electoral abuse by providing an incentive for incumbents to rig elections in their favor to avoid prosecution.
- INEC is not an independent body and succumbed to the pressure of the incumbent PDP.

The National Democratic Institute for International Affairs (NDI: 2008) on their own part, remarked that the Independent National Electoral Commission (INEC) failed to act upon shortcomings and recommendations that were identified a year before the 2007 election, with the result that polling stations in many states opened hours late, closed early or failed to open at all.

NDI also observed the following serious irregularities in the majority of states visited:

- failure to display the voter register;
- inadequate supplies of voting materials;
- ballot papers that did not include all of the candidates;
- inadequate locations and facilities for voting and collation;
- lack of secrecy of voting;
- disenfranchisement due to errors in the voter register ; and
- underage voting.

President Obasanjo himself admitted that the election was fraudulent. In a BBC interview, he stated as follows;

> I don't deny that there were imperfections in the elections, but the magnitude does not make the results null and void. We should not be measured by European standards. Nigeria has come a long way from when I first voted. We are better than 20 years ago.

International standards that were breached by the conduct of the 2007 general elections in Nigeria include Article 25 of the International Covenant on Civil and Political Rights (ICCPR), which Nigeria ratified in 1993, and Articles 3, 5, 6, 7 of the Economic Community of West African States' (ECOWAS) Protocol on Democracy and Good Governance, adopted in 2001. These provisions relate to, among others, relating to secrecy of the vote, universal franchise, independence and neutrality of the election administration, transparency and the disposal of petitions.

The 2007 general election was significant because for the first time since independence, the election would see power transferred from one civilian President to another thereby consolidating both the electoral process and Nigeria's nascent democracy. But whereas the peaceful transition in 1979 had made Obasanjo's reputation, the electoral fiasco of 2007 ruined it. As a result, he was denied a farewell visit to President Bush (Ilife: 2011).

4.2.0 Impact of Corruption on Nigerian Foreign Policy

The impact of corruption on Nigerian foreign policy identified in this section include loss of image; international isolation; lack of foreign direct investment/divestment; dwindling official development assistance; depletion of external reserves/accumulation of foreign debt; and harassment of Nigerians abroad.

4.2.1 Loss of Image

Shaukat Hassan as quoted in Ogwu (2005) notes that one of the negative consequences of corruption for state is loss of image. Corruption has without doubt tainted the image of a well-respected and responsible member of the international community, which Nigeria had always portrayed through its Afro-centrist foreign policy. This is evident from its consistent ranking by Transparency International as one of the most corrupt countries in the world.

The annual Corruption Perception Index (CPI) published by Transparency International ranks countries according to the level that corruption is perceived to exist among its politicians and bureaucrats. The CPI is based on multiple surveys of business people, the general public and country analyst by independent institutions conducted over a number of years. Countries are scored on a scale of 10 (least corrupt) to 0 (most corrupt).

Jude Uddoh, Ph.D.

Table 4.4 Five Most Corrupt Countries (1996 – 2006)

	1st	2nd	3rd	4th	5th
1996	Nigeria	Pakistan	Kenya	Bangladesh	China
1997	Nigeria	Bolivia	Columbia	Russia	Pakistan
1998	Cameroon	Paraguay	Honduras	Nigeria/ Tanzania	Indonesia
1999	Cameroon	Nigeria	Indonesia	Azerbaijan	Uzbekistan/ Honduras
2000	Nigeria	Yugoslavia	Ukraine/ Azerbaijan	Indonesia/ Angola	Cameroon
2001	Bangladesh	Nigeria	Uganda/ Indonesia	Kenya & 3 ors.	Ukraine
2002	Bangladesh	Nigeria	Paraguay & 2 ors.	Kenya/ Indonesia	Azerbaijan
2003	Bangladesh	Nigeria	Haiti	Paraguay/ Myanmar	Tajikistan & 4 ors.
2004	Haiti/ Bangladesh	Nigeria	Myanmar/ Chad	Paraguay/ Azerbaijan	Turkmenistan & 6 ors.
2005	Chad/ Bangladesh	Turkmenistan & 2 ors.	Nigeria & 3 ors.	Angola	Tajikistan & 6 ors
2006	Haiti	Myanmar & 2 ors.	Sudan & 3 ors.	Uzbekistan & 4 ors.	Nigeria & 9 ors.

Source: Transparency international www.transparency.org

Nigeria was first ranked as the most corrupt country in 1996 and 1997 respectively, during the regime of General Sani Abacha, thereafter dropping to fourth position in 1998. Nigeria was in second position in the CPI at the onset of the Obasanjo administration in 1999, climbing once more to the most corrupt country the following year (2000). Commenting on Nigeria's performance in the CPI (2000), Peter Eigen – Chairman of Transparency International, noted that;

> Valiant efforts are being made by President Olusegun Obasanjo to promote large-scale changes in a country whose people have been robbed by the grand corruption of their leaders. But, the process of change initiated by

the new President is barely 12 months old and so it is not surprising that Nigeria's CPI score is virtually unchanged (Eigen: 2000: 4).

Nigeria retained second position in the CPI in 2001, 2002, 2003 and 2004, after which it recorded steady improvements from third position in 2005 to fifth position in 2006. By the last year of the Obasanjo administration (2007), Nigeria's position in the CPI had further improved to ninth position (Table 4.4). Nigeria's cumulative average position in the CPI from 1996 to 2007 was 2.83.

According to the Vision 2010 Committee (Shonekan: 1997), the external image of any nation is how that nation is perceived by the outside world. On her own part, Ogwu (2005) locates a country's image as dwelling in the psychological realm, which is distinct, but nevertheless vital, together with other components of national power including military and economic strength. She further asserts that;

A major liability and burden on (Nigeria's) national image is the prevalence of corruption in the society. This has become universally established as a major characteristic of Nigeria in the past two decades.

Nigeria's image as a corrupt country is hinged on several practices prevalent in society, including graft and inflation of contracts, bribery, misappropriation or diversion of funds, kickbacks and over-invoicing, advance fee fraud, notoriously known in Nigeria as '419' and credit cards frauds abroad, among others.

A new dimension was added to Nigeria's tarnished image during the Obasanjo administration when a number of state governors – symbols of Nigeria's political authority and sovereignty, were paraded in foreign courts on corruption related charges. The list includes Governor Joshua Dariye of Plateau State, Governor D. S. P. Alamieyesegha of Bayelsa State, and Governor James Ibori of Delta State.

Nigeria's global image and reputation for corruption led to the corrosion of the country's presumed leadership position as the "giant of Africa." Jega (2010) surmised that Nigeria's leadership status in Africa is rather presumptuous as many phrases have emerged to describe Nigeria, in relationship to the rest of the world. They include "a nation of scammers," 'a crippled giant,' 'an open sore of the continent,' 'a giant with clay feet,' etc. (also Adebajo: 2008).

In the wake of massive corruption in both the home Ministry of Defence as well as the field operations of the Nigerian-led ECOMOG intervention in Liberia, Leatherwood (2001) reached the conclusion that;

> Nigeria, with its endemic corruption and other vestiges of its recent past, is not yet capable of instilling lasting stability in other countries.

4.1.2 International Isolation

Nigeria's growing reputation as one of the most corrupt countries in the world coupled with years of military rule and the antecedent human rights abuses was to drive the country to international isolation and pariah status.

Corruption is said to have become legitimized in Nigeria during the Babangida and Abacha regimes (1985-1998) which were characterized by huge revenues but wasteful spending, and nothing to show in terms of physical developments. Hence, Sowunmi et al (2010) make the point that;

> The culture of corruption through what Nigerians have come to know, as settlement syndrome became part of the country's political culture. All the positive values for development were jettisoned. Governmental agencies that were the pilots of socioeconomic developments were decimated.

Both Saliu (1999) and Osaghae (1998) agree that General Babangida's annulment of the 1993 election adjudged by domestic and international monitors as the freest and fairest in Nigeria's history more than any other singular event, catapulted Nigeria into the troubled waters of image crisis. The subsequent execution of Ken Saro-Wiwa and 8 other

Ogoni activists by General Sani Abacha, only carried global anger to a new height.

It was also during the regime of General Sani Abacha that Transparency International first ranked Nigeria as the most corrupt country in two consecutive years (1996 and 1997). As Abegunrin (2003: 154) surmises;

> Under Abacha, Nigeria became a haven for drug dealers, which together with other criminal activities by individuals abroad, such as 419 frauds, and the hanging of Ken Saro-Wiwa and his fellow Ogoni activists, made Nigeria a pariah in the eyes of the international community.

Nigeria's domestic polity characterized by endemic corruption and protracted military rule with attendant human rights abuse, combined to drive Nigeria into pariah status while its image took a turn for the worse. Nigeria was so much isolated that General Abacha's foreign policy described as "area boy diplomacy" was mostly reactionary and known for its by paranoia, hostility and defiance.

Fafowora (1997) contends that Nigeria's foreign policy and diplomacy were in disarray during the Abacha regime. Its role in international affairs was on the decline, while its global influence waned considerably. Nigeria was no longer a key player in each of the three main theaters of its traditional diplomacy – the United Nations (UN), the Commonwealth, and the Organization of African Unity (OAU). Several UN agencies including the Human Rights Commission and the International Labour Organization denounced and criticized Nigeria for its human rights abuses. Nigeria was suspended from the Commonwealth on account of the execution of the Ogoni nine in 1995, and the country's diplomatic relations with key Commonwealth countries such as Britain and Canada was at its lowest ebb. The European Union (EU), including Britain and the United States (US) imposed mandatory sanctions against Nigeria.

Nigeria suffered a major decline in its influence in Africa, which had always been the center of its foreign policy. Nigeria was no longer consulted by the key players in Africa, in spite of its major role in the liberation struggles of South Africa, Namibia, Zimbabwe, Angola and Mozambique. Nigeria was practically in a position of personam non grata in Africa. No African leader paid official visit to Nigeria. Nigeria was marginalized at the three concentric levels of its diplomacy.

Three events during the Abacha regime highlight Nigeria's increasing isolation in Africa. The first was usurpation of Nigeria's historical role in the Congo by South Africa on the outbreak of fresh crisis between Mobutu Sese Sekou and Joseph Kabila. Secondly was the state visit of Libyan leader – Muamar Gaddaffi, an international outcast to Nigeria, at a time when he was under a UN imposed air traffic ban. The third event was the moral dilemma presented by General Abacha's dispatch of Nigerian-led ECOMOG forces to restore the civilian democratic government of Tejan Kabba in Sierra Leone, while denying Nigerians at home the dividends of democracy. Fafowora (1997) makes the point on the international isolation of Nigeria thus;

> Real friendship and political alliances can only be constructed on the basis of mutuality of interests and shared values, which do not now exist between Nigeria and its traditional allies.

In his contribution to the Seminar on the Appraisal of the Social and Moral Image of the Nigerian Society jointly organized by the Kaduna State Government, the New Nigerian Newspapers Limited, and the Nigerian Television Authority from 7th – 9th June 1995 at Kaduna, Alhaji Adamu Ciroma lamented the international absurdities that Nigeria and Nigerian were subjected to such as the shifting of focus in economic events in Africa from Nigeria to other countries like Uganda, Kenya, and Ghana (Isa: 1995).

The isolation of Nigeria by the international community during the Abacha regime extended to the field of sports and specifically soccer, when FIFA – the world soccer governing body, cancelled the 8th World Youth Football Championship scheduled for Nigeria in 1995 on grounds of political instability and security concerns (Fawole: 1999). The Catholic Pontiff – Pope John Paul also joined in calling on General Abacha to end corruption and repressive rule, and demonstrate respect for human rights, during his visit to Nigerian in March 1998.

It was in the face of international isolation of Nigeria as a result of the country's record of endemic corruption and human rights abuse, that General Abacha sought for new friends from outside Nigeria's traditional friends and allies, including Libya, Iraq, Iran, North Korea and China, who historically had nothing in common with Nigeria, and who had little or nothing to offer Nigeria politically or economically.

4.2.3 Lack of Foreign Direct Investment and Divestment

A Harvard University research based on Transparency International's Corruption Perception Index (CPI) found that;

> A rise in corruption levels from that of Singapore to that of Mexico is equivalent to raising the marginal tax rate by over twenty per cent. A one percentage point increase in the marginal tax rate reduces inward foreign direct investment by about five per cent (Wei: 1998).

In other words, MNCs perceive corruption in host countries as the equivalent of tax increase and this has the effect of reducing FDI. Another research conducted among 50 U.S. and 71 European MNCs found that corruption as a risk factor inhibiting FDI outweighs other such considerations as human rights, environment, or labor issues (Bray: 1999).

Corruption in Nigeria historically accounts for lack of foreign direct investment (FDI) especially in the non-oil sector, and divestment from the country. UNCTAD (2009) notes that;

> Decades of political instability, economic mismanagement and endemic corruption further reduced Nigeria's ability to attract and retain FDI. This was compounded by a relentless deterioration of the country's social conditions and physical infrastructure, in spite of increased revenue generated by the oil sector.

General Babangida adopted economic diplomacy as the main thrust of his regime's foreign policy, which was partly aimed at halting divestment and increasing foreign direct investment into the country. Yet Professor Humphrey Asobie notes that Babangida's economic diplomacy did not accelerate the rate of net capital inflow to Nigeria, rather FDI remained sluggish and was mostly directed towards the oil sector while divestment plagued the industrial and manufacturing sectors during the Babangida regime. Over 150 multinational corporations (MNCs) divested from Nigeria since 1995, while more than 60 per cent of local industries, mostly small scale enterprises folded up since 1986, when the Structural Adjustment Programme (SAP) was introduced (Osaghae: 1998).

Another major constraint of Babangida's policy of economic diplomacy was the perpetuation of fraud in private sector business transactions;

> ...the issues of bad, sometimes fraudulent business practices by Nigerian exporters and businessmen, a phenomenon which has earned notoriety as 419 with consequent deleterious effect on the credibility of Nigerian operators within the international business community (Akinsanya et al: 1991: 132).

The Committee on 2010 set up by the General Sani Abacha had noted in its report that some of the consequences of Nigeria's poor external image is declining flow of foreign direct investment into the country and divestment from Nigeria (Shonekan: 1997). Foreign investors continued to shun Nigeria in spite of the repeal of two anti-FDI laws – the Exchange Control Act of 1962 and the Enterprises Promotion Decree of 1972 by the Abacha regime. Capital flight and divestment by foreign companies was the norm. MNCs that reduced their holdings in Nigeria between 1993 and 1994 include Standard Chartered bank, the Wellcome Foundation, and Unilever Plc (Osaghae: 1998).

Nigeria ranked below average in the 2005 Transparency International Business Confidence Survey among African countries surveyed (Table 4.5).

Table 4.5 Assessment of Market Attractiveness in Sub-Saharan Africa

Strategic Markets	Problematic Markets	
South Africa	Algeria	Angola
	Cameroun	Cote d'Ivoire
	Ghana	Kenya
	Morocco	Nigeria
	Tanzania	Tunisia
	Uganda	Zambia
	Zimbabwe	

Source: Nwankwo (2006)

The impact of advance fee fraud or "419" obtaining by false pretence practised by Nigerians has been particularly deleterious to Nigeria's efforts to attract FDI.

> The "419" advance fee fraud is one of the best known international financial scam which bilks hundreds of millions of dollars annually and contributes to worsening Nigeria's image internationally. Its pervasiveness had severe negative consequences on Nigeria. These include reduced FDI flows to the country and difficulties in business prospecting for genuine Nigerian business people, spurned by the international business community because of distrust (UNCTAD: 2009)

The common fear expressed by potential investors in the Nigerian economy is that, "ccorruption has so distorted Nigeria's business and investment climate that only the brave or those already tainted would think of doing business there (Ilife: 2011)." Multinational Corporations (MNCs) that divested from Nigeria during the Obasanjo administration include Michelin, Dunlop, Pfizer, Aventis, GlaxoWellcome and SmithKline Beecham (GlaxoSmithKline), Hoescht and Procter and Gamble (P&G).

4.2.4 Depletion of External Reserves/ Accumulation of Foreign Debt.

Historically, Nigeria's external debt was driven by corruption and the mismanagement of substantial oil revenue accruing to the country by the respective administrations. The former President of the World Bank – Paul Wolfowitz estimates that Nigeria lost over $300 billion to corruption between 1970 and 2001.

The profligacy of the Gowon regime in an era of oil boom left Nigeria with a debt burden of $1.6 billion. Beginning from 1977, the Federal Government under the Obasanjo regime resorted to heavy borrowing from the Western money market, without taming its own economy. The Shagari administration wiped out N2.3 billion external reserve it inherited as of 1979, and replaced it with a staggering external debt of N10.21 billion. Profligacy of the Second Republic politicians especially misuse of power by the law-makers was largely responsible for transforming Nigeria into a debtor nation (Agedah; 1993).

Part of General Babangida's foreign policy as outlined in his maiden speech of August 28, 1985 and includes resolving Nigeria's debt plight, and his administration's Structural Adjustment Programme (SAP) was directed primarily at among others, facilitating the rescheduling of Nigeria's external debts (Asobie: 1990). Yet, the same administration clandestinely disbursed almost $12.4 billion oil revenue windfall from the Gulf War while the country was openly reeling with a crushing external debt overhang.

Transparency International estimates that General Sani Abacha and his associates stole between $2 billion and $5 billion from the Nigeria treasury, placing him among the top 5 political looters of all time. Much of the interests and penalties accumulated on Nigeria's foreign debt are as a result of the refusal by Paris Club creditors to negotiate a debt workout with Nigeria's military dictators, including General Sani Abacha. This was in addition to a refusal by the major international financial institutions to endorse the economic plans of the regime.

The regime of General Abdulsalami Abubakar depleted the national treasury in unbudgeted and unaccounted for government expenditures.

The country's foreign reserve was depleted from $7.1 billion in January 1999 to $3.75 billion as of May 1999.

Table 4.6 Breakdown of Nigeria's External Debt (Dec. 2004)

Source	Amount (%)
Paris Club	85.82
Multinational sources	7.86
London Club	4.0
Promissory notes	2.18
Non-Paris bilateral	0.13

Source: DMO (2005)

As of December 2004, Nigeria owed a total of $35.994 billion with over 85% of the debt owed to the Paris Club (Table 4.6).

4.1.5 Harassment of Nigerians Abroad

The Committee on Vision 2010 outlined one of the consequences of Nigeria's poor external image as harassment of Nigerians in foreign countries by such local agencies as immigration, customs and the police, mostly on unwarranted suspicion (Shonekan: 1997). Similarly, Alhaji Adamu Ciroma – one time Governor of the Central Bank of Nigeria, lamented the international absurdities that Nigeria and Nigerian were subjected to, including the rough and unpleasant treatment Nigerians received from the customs and security officials of other countries based on the general assumption that all Nigerians were crooks (Isa: 1995).

In several reported instances, Nigerians were singled out from queues at international airports and kept waiting for hours or subjected to humiliating bodily searches. On numerous occasions, even Nigerian diplomats and diplomatic baggage were subjected to the same kind of treatment, clearly in breach of their diplomatic immunity and privileges and contrary to the respect that Nigerians were hitherto accorded all over Africa and the world at large.

Lamenting on the ill-treatment of Nigerian citizens abroad, General Babangida noted in his address during the NIIA annual patron's dinner in 1992 that;

> Nigeria's image in the world has been tainted partly as a result of an accustomed exaggeration of the involvement of Nigerians in drug peddling and perpetration of business fraud. It is true that some Nigerians have been thrown into foreign jails mainly for drug related offences but the number of people involved has always been exaggerated and thousands of innocent Nigerians have been ill-treated at different international airports. The situation has gone to the extent that every potential Nigerian traveler is suspected and seen as a drug pusher.

The Nigerian Government had lodged formal protests with the European Union (EU), the United Nations (UN) and other international organizations over the harassment of Nigerians in foreign lands. A Permanent Secretary in the Ministry of Foreign Affairs – Hakeem Baba Ahmed announced that a situation where security operatives harass Nigerians at entry points was unacceptable. He alleged that in most cases, it was only Nigerians that were being subjected to such inhuman treatment including the use of dogs to screen Nigerian males and females abroad, which besides its indignity, also has cultural and religious implications.

References
Chapter Four

Abdulah, Abdulwahab (2009) *My Friends Deserted Me in Prison* Interview with Bode George Vanguard February 18, 2911.

Abegunrin, Olayiwola (2003) *Nigerian Foreign Policy under Military Rule, 1966-1999* Westport, Praeger Publishers

Adebajo, Adekeye (2008) "Mad Dog and Glory: Nigeria's Intervention in Liberia and Sierra Leone" in Adebajo Adekeye and Mustapha Abdul Raufu (2008) *Gulliver's Trouble: Nigeria's Foreign Policy after the Cold War* South Africa, University of KwaZulu-Natal Press Pp. 177 – 202.

Adetula, Victor (Ed) (2008) *Money and Politics in Nigeria* Abuja, International Foundation for Electoral System

Agedah, Dickson (1993) *Corruption and the Stability of the Third Republic* Lagos, Perception Publications

Ajaero, Chris (2012) *Ibori's Long Road to Jail* Newswatch, May 13, 2012

Akinsanya, Olusegun et al (1991) *Nigeria's Economic Diplomacy (The Ike Nwachukwu Years, 1988 – 1992)* Nigeria, Ministry of Foreign Affairs

Andvig J. C. and Fjeldstad O. (2000) *Research on Corruption: A Policy Oriented Survey* Oslo, Norwegian Institute of International Affairs

Asobie, Asisi H. (1990) "Nigeria: Economic Diplomacy and National Interest. An Analysis of the Policies of Nigeria's External economic Relations, with Special Reference to Ibrahim Babangida's Administration. Paper presented at the 16th Annual Conference of the Nigerian Society of International Affairs. Lagos, NIIA Nov. 5 – 6, 1990. P. 20

Bray, J (1999) *Surveying Corruption,* London, Control Risks Group

Jude Uddoh, Ph.D.

Edwards Angell Palmer & Dodge (2008) *Recovering Stolen Assets: A Case Study* IBA Conference Paris, 24 – 25 April, 2008

Eigen, Peter (2000) *Transparency International Releases the Year 2000 Corruption Perception Index* TI Newsletter www.transparency.org

Ekeanyanwu Lillian, Loremikan Shina, Ikubaje John (2004) *The National Integrity System, TI Country Study Report, Nigeria 2004* Berlin, Transparency International

EU EOM (2007) *Nigeria: Presidential, National Assembly, Gubernatorial, and State House of Assembly Elections. Final Report* Abuja, European Union Election Observation Mission.

European Commission (2010) *Nigeria: Country Level Evaluation.* Final Report. Volume 1: Main Report.

Fafowora, Oladapo (1997) *Nigeria: Foreign Policy and Diplomatic Disarray* African Journal of International Affairs, Vol. 1, No. 1, 1997

House of Commons (2009) *DFID's Programme in Nigeria.* 8th Report of Session 2008-09 International Development Committee. London. The Stationay Office Ltd

HRW (2011) *Corruption on Trial? The Record of Nigeria's Economic and Financial Crimes Commission.* New York, Human Rights Watch.

IRI (2007) *Federal Republic of Nigeria State and National Elections April 14 and 21, 2007: Election Observation Final Report.* Washington DC, The International Republican Institute

Isa, Lawal J. (Ed) (1995) *Not in Our Character: Proceeding of the National Seminar on the Appraisal of the Social and Moral Image of the Nigerian Society* Kaduna, Kaduna State Government

Jega, Attahiru M. (2010) "Nigeria's Foreign Policy and the Promotion of Peace, Development, and Democracy," in Jega, Attahiru M. and

Farris, Jacqueline W. (Eds.) (2010) *Nigeria at Fifty: Contributions to Peace, Democracy and Development* Abuja, The Shehu Musa Yar'Adua Foundation

Leatherwood, David G. (2001) *Peacekeeping in West Africa* Joint Force Quarterly, Autumn-Winter, 2001

Ministry of Finance (2003) *The Nigerian Governance and Corruption Study.* Zaria, University of Zaria.

NDI (2008) *Final NDI Report on Nigeria's 2007 Elections* Washington DC, National Democratic Institute

Nuamah, Rosemary Rpt. (2003) *Nigeria's Foreign Policy after the Cold War: Domestic, Regional and External Influence.* UK, Oxford University Press

Nwabueze, Ben (2007) *How President Obasanjo Subverted the Rule of Law and Democracy* Ibadan, Gold Press Limited

Nwankwo, Adaora (2006) *The Determinants of Foreign Direct Investment Inflows (FDI) in Nigeria* 6th Global Conference on Business & Economics. Gutman Conference Center, USA

Obasanjo, Olusegun 1999, *Inaugural Speech* West Africa Review: 1, 1. www.icaap.org/iuicode?101.1.1.1Obasanjo: 2005

Ogwu, Joy (2005) *National Reputation and the Logic of Rebuilding Nigeria's Foreign Image* The Guardian October 20, 2005 Pg. 8

Osaghae, Eghosa E. (1998) *Crippled Giant: Nigeria since Independence* Bloomington, Indiana University Press

Peel, Michael (2006) *Nigeria-Related Financial Crime and Its Links with Britain.* Chattam House, London (UNODC: 2005).

Saliu, Hassan A. (1999) "Limitations of Nigerian Foreign Policy" in Aliu, Hasan A (Ed) (1999) *Selected Themes in Nigerian Foreign Policy and International relations* Ilorin, Sally and Associates pp. 121 – 140

Shoneka, E. A. O. (1997) *Vision 2010 Committee Report* Abuja, The Presidency

Sowunmi A, Raufu A. A, Oketokun F. O, Salako M. A, and Usifoh O. O, (2010) *The Role of Media in Curbing Corruption in Nigeria* Research Journal of Information Technology 2(1): 7-23, May 20, 2010

Transparency for Nigeria (2003) http://transparencyng.com/

UNCTAD (2009) *Nigeria: Investment Policy Review.* New York, United Nations Conference on Trade and Development

UNODC (2005) *Transnational Organized Crime in the West African Region.* Vienna, United Nations Office on Drugs and Crime

US Dept. of State (1997) *Nigerian Advanced Fee Fraud* Washington D.C., Bureau of International Narcotics and Law Enforcement Affairs

Wei, S (1998) *How Taxing is Corruption on International Investors?* USA, Harvard University

Chapter Five

NIGERIAN FOREIGN POLICY AND THE CHALLENGE OF CORRUPTION

The State shall abolish all corrupt practices and abuse of power. (S. 15 [5] Constitution of the Federal Republic of Nigeria 1999)

Corruption, the greatest single bane of our society today, will be tackled head-on at all levels (Obasanjo: 1999).

Introduction

In this Chapter, we will present an outline of President Olusegun Obasanjo's foreign policy as well as his administration's domestic reforms and anti-corruption institutions.

5.1.0 An Outline of President Olusegun Obasanjo's Foreign Policy

Section 19 in Chapter II of the Constitution of the Federal Republic of Nigeria 1999 operated by the Obasanjo administration, provides for the objectives of Nigerian foreign policy, as follows;

(a) Promotion and protection of the national interest;

(b) Promotion of African integration and support for African unity;

(c) Promotion of international cooperation for the consolidation of universal peace and mutual respect among all nations and elimination of discrimination in all its manifestations;

    (d) Respect for international law and treaty obligations as well as the seeking of settlement of international disputes by negotiation, mediation, conciliation, arbitration and adjudication; and

    (e) Promotion of a just world economic order.

When President Olusegun Obasanjo was sworn in on May 29, 1999 after nearly 16 years of military rule in Nigeria, he made it clear that there would be no radical shift in the country's external relations. Rather, Nigeria shall pursue a dynamic foreign policy to promote friendly relations with all nations and will continue to play a constructive role in the United Nations and the Organization of African Unity, and other international bodies. In his keynote address at the beginning of a retreat organized by the Presidential Advisory Council on International Relations (PAC), President Obasanjo reiterated that Africa should remain the centerpiece of the Nigerian foreign policy (Obasanjo: 2005: 16).

The philosophical foundation of Obasanjo's foreign policy was variously expounded by his foreign affairs ministers – Alhaji Sule Lamido (1999 – 2003), as "foreign policy for democracy" project, and under Olu Adeniji (2003 – 2006) as "beneficial concentricism" approach. The "foreign policy for democracy" project is underlined by the logic that democracy must provide concrete dividends (dividends of democracy) for the people within the shortest possible time (Ezea: 2000). The "beneficial concentricism" approach, on the other hand aims to make Nigerians the primary beneficiary of the country's foreign policy by weaving economic gains into the expenditures and thrusts of Nigeria's foreign policy (Adeniji: 2005).

The major thrusts and exertions of President Obasanjo's foreign policy were directed towards four priority areas, namely; redeeming Nigeria's image, recovery of looted funds stashed abroad, campaigning for debt relief, and attracting foreign direct investment (Abegunrin: 2006). All four priority areas were aimed at remedying damages that corruption had inflicted on Nigeria's image and economy.

5.1.1 International Image Laundering Efforts

President Obasanjo acknowledged in his inaugural speech that the impact of official corruption is so rampant and has earned Nigeria a very bad image at home and abroad; "Nigeria, once a well-respected country and a key role player in international bodies, became a pariah nation." He affirmed the resolve of his administration to restore Nigeria fully to her previous prestigious position in the comity of nations. The Obasanjo administration adopted several strategies to launder the image acquired by Nigeria as one of the most corrupt countries including shuttle diplomacy, official propaganda, and anti-corruption policy measures.

5.1.2 Shuttle Diplomacy

Even before his inauguration, Obasanjo visited over twenty foreign countries. By October 2002, Obasanjo had travelled to 92 countries as President, spending more than a quarter of his first term out of the country. President Obasanjo justified his frequent trips abroad in the following terms;

> This is a country that has been isolated, this is a country that needs to come into the mainstream of the international community, and …you don't sit at home to do that, you need to go round and say well look, we have a new Nigeria and I'm the epitome of that new Nigeria (Ilife: 2011).

Between May 1999 when President Obasanjo took office and August 2002, he travelled out of the country 113 times, and as at June 2002 he had been out of the country for a period of 340 days. The President's frequent trips abroad dubbed "Ajala" diplomacy enabled him to address world leaders at bilateral levels – in South Africa, the United States, France, and Britain, as well as in multilateral fora, including the United Nations (UN), Economic Community of West African States (ECOWAS), the

Group of 8 (G-8), Group 77 (G-77) the Commonwealth, African Union (AU) and European Union (EU).

Part of the objectives of Obasanjo's frequent trips abroad was restoration of Nigeria's image, which was battered by nearly 16 years of military rule, human rights abuse, and corruption. These overseas trips were significant for 2 major reasons. First is that they symbolized Nigeria's transition from the status of a pariah state when its leaders and their associates were isolated and denied travel visas by a host of foreign countries, to a new era of acceptance and reintegration into the comity of nations. Secondly, summit meetings are the highest form of diplomacy, enabling President Obasanjo to forcefully put across the challenges facing Nigeria, as well as his administration's efforts to address them before the international audience and to extract commitments from them, on a one-on-one basis.

President Obasanjo scored his administration a pass mark in its efforts to redeem Nigeria's image and reintegrate the country into the comity of nations;

> I have devoted much time and energy journeying virtually all corners of the globe in my personal effort to positively reintegrate our country into the international community and attract investment. We are happy to report that the results from these trips have been encouraging enough to confirm my personal belief and the advice of marketing experts, namely that personal contact is the best way to market your product. And my product is Nigeria (Obasanjo: 2002).

The opposing view is that Obasanjo could have still achieved the same objectives for which he frequently travelled abroad at home by working to improve domestic conditions such as security, infrastructure, deregulation and anti-corruption policy measures (Saliu: 2005).

5.1.3 Official Propaganda

The Vision 2010 Committee listed the determinants of a nation's image as including the content and effectiveness of its external propaganda (Shoneka: 1997). In 2004, the administration of President Olusegun Obasanjo government through the Federal Ministry of Information and National Orientation launched "The Nigerian Image Project," through which it aimed to promote national pride and present a positive image of Nigeria abroad. The Project which had Mr. Pascal Dozie as its Chairman received an initial government contribution of 6 billion (about $3 million), with the expectation that the private sector will also contribute towards the project as part of their corporate social responsibility.

The Nigerian Image Project which was originally planned as an informational and orientation campaign was renamed the Heart of Africa (HOA) Project in 2005 by then Minister of Information and Culture – Mr. Frank Nweke Jr. According to the Information Minister;

> The "Heart of Africa" project is a major effort by the government to reinvent our image and correct the very grave misrepresentation of our country and people by the Western media. Nigeria has acquired criminal connotations over time, on account, perhaps, of the activities of an insignificant number of compatriots. The activities of these insignificant few should not be allowed to stain the image of an otherwise vibrant country that holds so much promise (Nweke Jr: 2005).

The Project was launched in London on September 10, 2005 and in New York on October 14, 2005. The objective of launching the Project in major cities of the world is to gain access to large Nigerian populations as well as the western media in order to enlighten them on the efforts of Government. In March 2009, the Minister of Information and Communication – Dr. Dora Akunyili introduced the national slogan of "Good People Great Nation" during the launching of the re-branding Nigeria campaign.

The attempt to launder Nigeria's image through official propaganda was widely criticized as a "whitened sepulcher" approach that could not be sustained without frontally and objectively addressing those issues that gave Nigeria a bad name.

The Obasanjo administration understood that the objective and strategies for restoring and sustaining a positive image for Nigeria must necessarily begin with getting the fundamentals at home right, since the external image of a country is always a reflection of her domestic state of affairs. Hence it included the agenda for tackling corruption and promoting transparency and accountability in its development blueprint - the National Economic Empowerment and Development Strategy (NEEDS) In his forward to the NEEDS document President Obasanjo acknowledged that;

> Given the adverse implications of the negative values of a small number of people on the nation's image, growth, and development, the government cannot ignore them, particularly as experience has shown that the successful pursuit of a national vision has often been nurtured and advanced by the inculcation of good moral and ethical values in the citizenry (NPC: 2004).

President Obasanjo demonstrated his personal commitment to tackling corruption and increasing transparency, through a number of initiatives including the Independent Corrupt Practices and Other Related Crimes Commission (ICPC); the Economic and Financial Crimes Commission (EFCC); the Budget Monitoring and Price Intelligence Unit (Due Process); and the Extractive Industries Transparency Initiative (NEITI) as discussed in the subsequent sections below.

Table 5.1 Nigeria's Corruption Perception Index (1999 – 2007)

Year	1999	2000	2001	2002	2003	2004	2005	2006	2007
Ranking	2nd	1st	2nd	2nd	2nd	2nd	3rd	5th	9th

Source: Transparency International <u>www.transparency.org</u>

Through the various economic and anti-corruption reforms and other policy measures of the Obasanjo administration, Nigeria's ranking in the CPI improved from most corrupt country in 2000 to ninth position in the last year of the administration (Table 5.1). The former Secretary-General of the Commonwealth – Chief Emeka Anyaoku credits the Obasanjo administration with improving Nigeria's mage, and reintegrating the country into the comity of nations;

> Since 1999, Nigeria under our current President has reversed the international isolation to which we had been consigned as a result of our domestic situation which was characterized by major negations of the tenets of good governance. We are no longer a pariah state. We are now consulted on the major issues facing humanity, such as peace and stability in Africa, economic development, the environment and terrorism (Anyaoku: 2005:7).

5.2.0 Economic Diplomacy

President Obasanjo's pursuit of economic diplomacy is hinged on three focal points – recovery of looted funds stashed abroad by former Head of State General Sani Abacha and his associates; campaign for debt forgiveness; and attraction of foreign direct investment into the country (Saliu and Omotola: 2005).

5.2.1 Recovery of the Abacha Loot

At the 54th session of the UN General Assembly held in New York in September 1999, President Obasanjo called for international action to repatriate monies stolen from Africa and the developing world. He noted that;

> It is an open secret that much of Africa's wealth has been illegally siphoned out of the continent by corrupt

regimes and unpatriotic individuals working in collaboration with foreign partners. In this regard, Nigeria calls for a concerted effort by the international community, through an international convention, for the repatriation to Africa and the developing world of all capital illegally transferred from these countries (United Nations: 1999:10).

General Abdulsalaami Abubakar had initiated the process of recovering funds stolen by General Sani Abacha with the promulgation of Decree No. 53 of 1999 which facilitated the domestic recovery of $800 million in cash and assets from the Abacha family and associates.

In September 1999, the new administration of President Olusegun Obasanjo engaged a Swiss legal firm, Monfrini and Partners, to assist with tracing and recovering of monies held abroad. Swiss authorities accepted a request for Mutual Legal Assistance on December 1999, leading to the issuance of a general freezing order. It took Nigeria five years to obtain a repatriation decision from the Swiss authorities due to numerous appeals brought by the Abachas.

On February 7, 2005 the Federal Supreme Court of Switzerland authorized the repatriation by Switzerland to Nigeria of funds deposited by the Abacha family in Switzerland. The actual repatriation took place in 2005 ($461.3 million) and in 2006 ($44.1 million). A last small transfer of $5.2 million was made in August 2006. The total amount received by the Federal Government of Nigeria was equivalent to $505.5 million.

As a part of repatriation process, the Nigerian Governments, and the World Bank, agreed for a study to be carried out to analyze the use of the repatriated funds under the Public Expenditure Management and Financial Accountability Review (PEMFAR) as part of the Country Partnership Strategy (CPS). With a $280,000 grant from the Swiss government, the World Bank mobilized a coalition of Nigerian civil society organizations under the aegis of the Nigerian Network on Stolen Assets (NNSA) to participate in the review and analysis of the use of the looted funds.

Table 5.2 Utilization of Abacha Funds (N billions)

1.	Power (Rural Electrification and Power Generation)	21.70
2.	Works (Priority Economic Roads)	18.60
3.	Health (Primary Health and Vaccination Programmes)	10.83
4.	Education (Secondary and Basic Education)	7.74
5.	Water (Potable Water and Rural Irrigation)	6.20
	Total	65.07

Source: TWB/FMF (2006)

The stated purpose for the money was for funding the key sectors of Power (N21.70 billion); Roads (N18.60 billion); Health (N10.83); Education (N7.74 billion); and Water (N6.20 billion) (Table 5.2). The projects were spread across the 6 geo-political regions of Nigeria. They were carried out in the framework of Government's National Economic Empowerment and Development Strategy (NEEDS) as part of its Millennium Development Goals (MDG)

The World Bank/Federal Ministry of Finance monitoring team on the utilization of the Abacha funds notes three major challenges in their assigned task:

The repatriated Abacha loot were treated as part of general budget resources and not distinguished in any way from other budget spending.

1. Although the Abacha loot was actually repatriated to the Nigerian treasury in 2005 and 2006, the funds were retroactively spent as part of the budget for 2004.
2. There were a number of instances in which spending agencies used their share of the Abacha loot to either defray outstanding contractor arrears or to make partial payments for ongoing multi-year projects.
3. Overall, the Monitoring Team observed that of the 51 projects reviewed, 23 were described as "completed", 26 were at various stages of completion, and 2 were described as "abandoned" (TWB/FMF: 2006).

The shadow Report of the Nigerian Network on Stolen Assets (NNSA) examined a total of 54 projects out of which 29 were incomplete, 24 were completed and 1 could not be verified. NNSA noted in their Report that some contractors completed their assigned tasks properly and in good time, while some other completed projects exhibited such poor workmanship that the installation already required major refurbishing shortly after construction's completion.

The NNSA Report also observed that some projects were completed before 2004, making it doubtful whether the Abacha loot was actually applied towards their completion. NNSA advanced reasons for the non-completion of some of the projects as faults on the part of the FGN, faults on the part of contractors, faults on the part of the end users, and faults not attributable to any party (Ugolor et al: 2006).

5.2.2 Campaign for Debt Relief

As of December 2004, Nigeria owed the Paris Club $36 billion which represents about 85% of its foreign debt (Table 5.3). Britain held 75% of Nigeria's Paris Club debt ($8 billion) followed by France ($6.2 billion) and Germany ($5.2 billion). Britain held 75% of Nigeria's Paris Club debt ($8 billion) followed by France ($6.2 billion) and Germany ($5.2 billion).

Table 5.3 Breakdown of Nigeria's Paris Club Debt Stock ($ million)

1.	UK	8000.32
2.	France	6249.61
3.	Germany	5288.66
4.	Japan	4447.97
5.	Italy	1975.94
6.	Netherland	1707.98
7.	U.S.A.	984.49
8.	Belgium	608.19
9.	Denmark	571.75
10.	Austria	521.38

11.	Spain	249.54
12.	Switzerland	201.01
13.	Russian Federation	36.97
14.	Finland	3.99

Source: DMO (2005)

President Obasanjo had lamented the difficulties which external debts posed to the socio-economic development of Nigeria at various international fora, calling for debt remission from the industrialized nations beyond the highly indebted poor countries (HIPC) guidelines. In his address as Chairman of the G-77 at the South-South Summit held in Havanna Cuba in April 2000, President Obasanjo noted that;

> The heavy external debt burden and large unsustainable debt service obligations constitute a major obstacle to social and economic development, the fight against poverty, human security and stable democratic governance.

As Chairman of the African Union (AU), President Obasanjo had warned during the celebration of Africa Day at UNESCO that debt is "a direct obstacle to growth and development and, by implication, an obstacle to democratic consolidation." He also took the message of debt relief to the summit meeting between developing countries and the G-8 hosted by Japan. In his address to the International Labour Organization (ILO) in June 2005, Obasanjo insisted that "We are serious about reform and about building new paths to growth and development, but without debt relief these would be impossible."

In 2005, Britain acting as chair of the G-8 brought to the fore Third World, and particularly African debt issues. The G-8 in its communique recognized the progress made by Nigeria in the implementation of economic and governance reforms, and agreed to support a sustainable debt treatment for the country within the framework of the Paris Club.

At their meeting in June 2005, the Paris Club creditors announced the decision in principle to grant a debt relief package of $18 billion out of the $30.84 billion outstanding. Nigeria achieved about 60% cancellation of its Paris Club debt under the deal amounting to about $18 billion. Britain received $3 billion from the deal having cancelled $5 billion.

The Paris Club debt deal struck by the Obasanjo administration in 2005 by which Nigeria achieved about 60% cancellation of its debts was mainly as a result of the administration's concerted efforts at tackling corruption. Nigeria clearly did not qualify for debt relief under the highly indebted poor countries initiative (HIPC) launched in 1996 by the International Monetary Fund (IMF) and World Bank, with the aim of ensuring that no poor country faces a debt burden it cannot manage. The Head of Good Governance Section of the European Commission delegation to Nigeria – Marc Friedrich, notes that;

> Although there were many factors that would have contributed to the Paris club's decision but government's efforts at tackling corruption was one major factor the club considered (Reiffel: 2005).

President Obasanjo's international quest for debt reduction coupled with his domestic economic reforms as well as his anti-corruption policy measures were regarded as being instrumental to the Paris Club debt deal.

5.2.3 Attracting Foreign Direct Investment (FDI)

Corruption in both public and private sectors of the Nigerian economy not only hampers development, but also increases the cost of doing business. The 419 brand of international financial scam in particular contributed to further deterioration in Nigeria's image as well as engendering much mistrust for Nigerians among the international business community.

Historically, corruption was responsible for Nigeria's lack of foreign direct investment (FDI) and divestment. Hence, a major focus of the Obasanjo administration's economic diplomacy was the reversal of this trend by creating an environment that is conducive to the inflow of FDI into the country.

The Obasanjo administration adopted a home-grown model of comprehensive national development plan known as the National Economic Empowerment and Development Strategy (NEEDS), with principal focus in four key areas:

- Reorientating values
- Reducing poverty
- Creating wealth, and
- Generating employment.

FDI inflow into Nigeria from 1999 to 2009 totaled $21.149 billion baring incomplete data from 2006 (Table 5.4). Oil and gas accounted for 79% of the FDI while non-oil sector accounted for 21% investment. North America including USA and Canada was responsible for the largest portion of the FDI at $1,227.53 million, followed by Europe with $$9,044.67 million, and Africa ($538.91 million).

Table 5.4 FDI Inflow to Nigeria 1999 – 2006 ($mn)

Region	1999	2000	2001	2002	2003	2004	2005	2006*	Total
North America	7.35	9.84	12.10	36.16	40.34	4,354.14	5,166.32	1601.28	11,227..53
South America	1.15	2.96	0.39	0.06	7.14	60.04	24.56	11.76	108.05
Asia/ Pacific	2.94	5.93	4.45	5.17	1.54	32.12	47.2904	39.63	139.07
Middle/ Far East	7.41	2.75	10.29	5.3	6.74	23.27	21.215	13.39	90.995
Europe	164.95	136.452	98.86	200.24	293.66	2,624.30	3,084.68	2,441.52	9,044.67
Africa	6.79	9.45	8.24	24.3	91.41	173.62	169.04	56.06	538.91
	190.59	167.39	13.96	271.22	440.83	7,267.49	8,513.11	4,163.64	21,149.23

* 2006 data incomplete

Source: Nigerian Investment Promotion Commission (NIPC)

FDI inflow to Nigeria was in a flux for the better part of Obasanjo's first term in office, fluctuating from $190.59 million in 1999 to $167.39 million in 2000, and from $13.96 million in 2001 to $271.22 million in 2002. This was as a result of several factors including poor governance and corruption, weak infrastructure and lack of security, which made it difficult for the country to increase the rate of FDI inflows. However, FDI inflow into Nigeria improved substantially during the second term of the Obasanjo administration, increasing from $440.83 million in 2003 to $7,267.49 million in 2004 and further to $8,513.11 million in 2005 (Table 5.4).

5.3.0 Domestic Reforms and Anti-Corruption Institutions

None of Obasanjo's foreign policy priorities – image laundering, recovery of looted funds, campaign for debt remission and attraction of foreign direct investment (FDI), could have been possible without a comprehensive package of internal and external anti-corruption reform measures. Domestic reforms and anti-corruption institutions undertaken by the Obasanjo administration include the Independent Corrupt Practices and other related Offences Commission (ICPC); the Economic and Financial Crimes Commission (EFCC); the Budget Monitoring and Price Intelligence Unit (Due Process); the Nigerian Extractive Industries Transparency Initiative (NEITI); and the Nigerian Code of Conduct Bureau/Tribunal.

5.3.1 The Independent Corrupt Practices and other Related Offences Commission (ICPC)

The Independent Corrupt Practices and Other Related Offences Act 2000 came into force on 13 June 2000. On the occasion of the signing into law of the Act, President Olusegun Obasanjo reiterated the fight against corruption as the number one priority of his administration. He recounted the damage done by corruption to every facet of the Nigerian society including its external image and vowed to apply the same standard in bringing both Nigerians and foreigners alike who violate the anticorruption law to book.

The Anti-corruption Act is arranged into eight parts and 70 sections. Part 1 deals with preliminary matters, while Part 2 deals with establishment of the Independent Corrupt Practices and other Related

Offences Commission ("the Commission"), appointments and powers. Part 3 creates offences and penalties under the Act. Part 4 makes provisions concerning investigation, search, seizure and arrests. Part 5 contains other provisions relating to the chairman of the Commission. Part 6 deals with evidence. Part 7 outlines the process of prosecution and trial of offences, while Part 8 contains general provisions.

The 3 main responsibilities of the Commission as outlined in Section 6 (a-f) of the Act are:

- To receive and investigate reports of corrupt offences as created by the Act and in appropriate cases prosecute the offender(s) – Enforcement duties;
- To examine, review and enforce the correction of corruption-prone systems and procedures of public bodies, with a view to eliminating or minimizing corruption in public life – Prevention duties;
- To educate and enlighten the public on and against corruption with a view to enlisting and fostering public support for the fight against it – Education duties.

Other highlights of the Act, which President Obasanjo describes as "… the toughest anti-corruption law in the history of our nation," include Section 52 which creates the office of independent counsel to investigate the President or Vice-President of the Federation, the Governor or Deputy-Governor of a State, as well as the Chief Justice of Nigeria, under appropriate circumstances.

The Commission charged a total of 104 persons in 49 criminal cases to court within its first five years of inception. The accused persons include former local government chairmen and councilors, judges, magistrates and lawyers, police officers and other law enforcement officials, as well as legislators including former Senate President – Chief Adolphus Wabara.

By the end of President Obasanjo's administration in 2007, the Commission had secured only 20 convictions out of the 127 criminal cases against 241 individuals.

Table 5.5 ICPC Summary of Budgetary Proposal Released (%)

Fiscal Year	Capital	Personnel	Overhead
*2000			
2001	45.29	34.34	34.26
2002	Nil	13.38	8.07
2003	Nil	61.13	56.76
2004	49	75	41

Source: ICPC (2005)

*Take-off grant released to the Commission in 2000 was 17.17% of its proposal.

The biggest problem facing the Commission has been that of shortage of funds. Money was not allocated for the Commission in the 2000 budget as at the time it was set up, thus inhibiting the Commission from employing staff. The Commission has been consistently underfunded for capital, personnel and overhead expenditures from inception (see Table 5.5). For two consecutive years 2002 and 2003, the Commission received zero budgetary allocation for capital expenditure. This seriously inhibits the ability of the Commission to carry out its statutory functions. Poor funding of the ICPC suggests that Government set it up in order to appear to be doing something about corruption without considering the long-term resource implications, or it could also be as a result of Government's low-prioritization of its work (Theobold: 2000).

5.3.2 The Economic and Financial Crimes Commission (EFCC)

The Economic and Financial Crimes Commission (Establishment) Act No. 5, 2002 came into effect on 14 December 2002. The Act contains seven parts made up of 41 sections.

Part 1 of the Act provides for establishment of the Economic and Financial Crimes Commission ("the Commission") and related matters, while Part 2 outlines the functions of the Commission. Part 3 deals with staffing of the Commission. Part 4 outlines offences punishable under the Act, while Part 5 deals with forfeiture of assets of persons arrested for offences under the Act. Part 6 contains financial provisions, and Part 7 deals with other miscellaneous provisions.

The Commission is responsible for the investigation of all financial crimes including advance fee fraud, money laundering, counterfeiting, illegal charge transfers, futures market fraud, fraudulent encashment of negotiable instruments, computer credit card fraud, contract scam, etc.

Section 6(1) of the Act provides for special powers of the Commission. It states that the Commission has power to –

(a) Cause investigations to be conducted as to whether any person has committed an offence under this Act; and

(b) With a view to ascertaining whether any person has been in offences under this Act or in the proceeds of any such offences, cause investigations to be conducted into the properties of any person if it appears to the Commission that the person's lifestyle and extent of the properties are not justified by his source of income.

The Commission is charged with the specific responsibility of enforcing the following provisions:

(a) The Money Laundering Act 1995;

(b) The Advance Fee Fraud and Other Related Offences Act 1995;

(c) The Failed Banks (Recovery of Debts) and Financial Malpractices in Banks Act 1994, as amended;

(d) The Banks and Other Financial Institutions Act 1991, as amended;

(e) Miscellaneous Offences Act; and

(f) Any other law or regulation relating to economic and financial crime.

In addition to the foregoing, section 11(1) of the Act establishes several special units of the Commission which include the General and Assets Investigation Unit S.11 (1) (a), and the Legal and Prosecution Unit S.11 (1) (b). These special units are charged with specific responsibilities with regard to the work of the Commission.

Since its inception in 2003, The EFCC has recovered about US$11 billion proceeds of crime. Between June 2008 and March 2011, the EFCC recovered $4.3 billion from banking sector reforms; $903.3 million from assets forfeiture, advance fee fraud etc.; $240 million from penalties imposed on MNCs; $10 million from local businesses; and $23 million from tax evasion.

Since 2005, the EFCC has arraigned 30 nationally prominent political figures on corruption charges, but many of the corruption cases against the political elite have made little progress in the courts (Table 5.6). Only four convictions of nationally prominent political figures were obtained by the EFCC in eight years (2003 – July 2011), namely Tafa Balogun (former Inspector General of Police), Diepreye Alamieyesegha (former Goivernor of Bayelsa State), Lucky Igbinedion (former Governor of Edo State) and Olabode George (prominent member of the ruling PDP and former Chairman, Nigerian Ports Authority). Out of this number, only one conviction (Olabode George) was obtained at trial while the other three were obtained through plea bargain.

Table 5.6 Ten Nationally Prominent Political Figures Charged by the EFCC (April 2003 – December 2007)

	Defendant	Office Held	Date Charged
1.	Tafa Balogun	Inspector General of Police (2002-2005)	April 2005
2.	Diepreye Alamieyesegha	Governor of Bayelsa State (1999-2007)	December 2006
3.	Abubakar Audu	Governor of Kogi State (1999-2003)	July 2007
4.	Joshua Dariye	Governor of Plateau State (1999-2007)	July 2007
5.	Orji Kalu	Governor of Abia State (1999-2007)	July 2007
6.	Saminu Turaki	Governor of Jigawa State (1999-2007)	July 2007
7.	Jolly Nyame	Governor of Taraba State (1999-2007)	July 2007

8.	Chimaroke Nnamani	Governor of Enugu State (1999-2007)	July 2007
9.	James Ibori	Governor of Delta State (1999-2007)	December 2007
10.	Ayo Fayoshe	Governor of Ekiti State (2003-2006)	December 2007

Source: HRW (2011)

The EFCC was accused of being selective in its investigation and prosecution of offenders, and of being used by President Obasanjo to harass his political opponents (Ploch: 2008). Again, the independence of the EFCC is compromised by Section 3(2) of the Act which provides as follows:

> The Chairman and members of the Commission may at any time be removed by the President for inability to discharge the functions of his office (whether arising from infirmity of mind or body or any other cause) or for misconduct or if the President is satisfied that it is not in the interest of the Commission or the interest of the public that the member should continue in office.

Two former chairmen of the EFCC – Nuhu Ribadu and Farida Waziri were removed from office pursuant to this provision. Other problems militating against the EFCC include lack of support from ancillary bodies, primarily that of the Attorney General of the Federation under the tenure of Michael Andoakaa, when he was alleged to have compromised a number of EFCC's most prominent cases including that of James Ibori – former Governor of Delta State. Other shortcomings include judicial inefficiency, delay and compromise, error and incompetence on the part of the EFCC itself (HRW: 2011).

In spite of its shortcomings, the EFCC has been hailed as "…the most successful anti-corruption agency in Africa (which) helped Nigeria reach the 147th position in Transparency International's Corruption Perception Index from last in 2003 and third to last in 2005" (UNODC: 2008).

5.3.3 Budget Monitoring and Price Intelligence Unit (Due Process)

The Budget Monitoring and Price Intelligence Unit (BMPIU) also known as "Due Process" was established by the Obasanjo administration in 2001. The objectives of BMPIU are;

1. To harmonize existing government policies/practices and update same on public procurement.
2. To determine whether or not Due Process has been observed in the procurement of services and contracts
3. To introduce more honesty, accountability and transparency into the procurement process
4. To establish and update pricing standards and benchmarks for all supplies to Government
5. To monitor the implementation of projects during execution with a view to providing information on performance, output and compliance with specifications and targets
6. To ensure that only projects which have been budgeted for are admitted for execution.

BMPIU carries out regulatory, monitoring, training and advisory functions as well. The BMPIU sets the following criteria for approval of contracts:

- Contracts below N1million may be approved by the Permanent Secretary or Chief Executive of parastatals.
- Contracts over N1million but below N50million are to be approved by Resident Due Process Team (RDPT).
- Contracts above N50million are to be considered by the Ministerial Tender Board (MTB) and forwarded to BMPIU to obtain a Due Process Certificate for approval by the Federal Executive Council.

In addition to the foregoing, projects below N10million are required to be posted at the relevant Notice Boards of the procurement agency while projects above N10million must be advertised in at least two national newspapers including Federal Tenders Journal or government gazette.

BMPIU was transformed into The Public Procurement Act 2007 which essentially replaced the obsolete Finance Act of 1958. The objectives of the Public Procurement Act include,

> … to ensure the equal treatment of companies during public procurement, encourage efficiency in public operations through active competition and promote innovation and development in the public procurement of goods, labour and services.

The Public Procurement Act established the National Council on Public Procurement and the Bureau of Public Procurement as the regulatory authorities responsible for the monitoring and oversight of public procurement, harmonizing the existing government policies and practices by regulating, setting standards and developing the legal framework and professional capacity for Public Procurement in Nigeria; and other related matters.

According to President Obasanjo the Due Process mechanism process initiated by his administration saved Nigeria over N102 billion in two years, arising from various over-bloated Federal Government contracts. Also, the Senior Special Assistant to the President on BMPIU, Dr. (Mrs.) Oby Ezekwesili disclosed that her office saved N672.4 million from a single project by the Ministry of Health meant to procure and supply equipment to tertiary health institutions in the country (Adenirokun: 2004). The BMPIU was plagued by several problems including bureaucratic delays.

5.3.4 Nigerian Extractive Industries Transparency Initiative (NEITI)

NEITI is the national version of the Extractive Industries Transparency Initiative (EITI) – essentially a voluntary disclosure code, launched by former British Prime Minister Tony Blair in 2002. EITI has the main objective of increasing transparency over payments by companies and revenues to governments in the extractive industries. The Initiative is expected to rescue countries like Nigeria whose population at large continue to live below the poverty line in spite of the country's rich oil and mineral resources.

The Nigerian Extractive Industries Transparency Initiative (NEITI) Act 2007 is charged with the responsibility, among other things, of the development of a framework for transparency and accountability in the reporting and disclosure by all extractive industry companies of revenue due to or paid to the Federal Government. NEITI also ensures transparency and accountability by government in the application of resources from payments received from the extractive industry companies.

The NEITI Act provides for the establishment of the National Stakeholders Workshop Group (NSWG) which is the governing body for NEITI. The NSWG is responsible for the formulation of policy, programs and strategies for the effective implementation of the functions of NEITI. Its membership comprises a chairman and 14 other members including an executive secretary who are constituted by the president. The NSWG reports to the President and National Assembly.

The Act provides for the offence of false statement of account or failure to render a statement of account by an extractive industry company, and a penalty upon conviction of a fine of not less than N30,000,000, a term of imprisonment of not less than 2 years for every Director or other person concerned, in addition to payment of the actual amount of revenue due to government. The President may also on the recommendation of the NSWG suspend or revoke the operational license of any such extractive industry company.

The audit report presented to NSWG by Hart Nurse Ltd in association with SS Afemikhe & Co for the period of 1999 to 2004 (Hart Group: 2006), show several shortcomings in the operation of NEITI. According to the report, several companies presented incorrect or omitted some transactions and there were some discrepancies between financial reports by some companies and government records. Deficiencies were also observed in the notification made to Auditor-General of Nigeria by paying entities and actual receipt by Central Bank of Nigeria. The auditors recommended regular reconciliation of export lifting between Department of Petroleum Resources and companies.

5.3.5 Nigerian Code of Conduct Bureau/Tribunal

The Code of Conduct for public officers is spelt out in Part 1 of the fifth Schedule to the 1999 Constitution of the Federal Republic of Nigeria. Its function includes;

> To establish and maintain a high standard of morality in the conduct of government business, and to ensure that the actions and behavior of public officers conform to the highest standards of public morality and accountability.

Section 11(1) provides inter alia;

Every public officer shall within 3 months after taking office and thereafter:

(a) at the end of every four years; and
(b) at the end of his term of office

Submit to the Code of Conduct Bureau a written declaration of all his properties, assets and liabilities and those of his spouse, or unmarried children under the age of 21 years.

A Code of Conduct Tribunal is empowered under the Constitution to punish any public officer found guilty of contravening any of the provisions of the Act. The Obasanjo administration overhauled the operations of the Code of Conduct Bureau and vested it with the power to investigate complaints. The Bureau, through its Department of Investigation and Monitoring, receives complaints of breaches of the code of conduct by public officers from members of the public. The complaints range from indiscipline, abuse of office, lack of accountability and corruption to unethical conduct in government business, among others.

Between 2000 and 2005, the Bureau secured a total of 2,380 convictions out of 4,656 cases which it forwarded to the Code of Conduct Tribunal for trial while 103 cases were either discharged or acquitted. A further unspecified number of cases were adjourned within this period (Table 5.7). Prior to the Obasanjo administration, the Code of Conduct Bureau was largely dormant and ineffective in the investigation of cases of breaches of the Code of Conduct for public officers.

Table 5.7 Code of Conduct Bureau Cases for Prosecution (2000 – 2005)

YEAR	NO. OF CASES TRIED	NO. CONVICTED	NO. DISCHARGED/ ACQUITED	NO. ADJOURNED
2000	416	235	15	166
2001	970	411	5	554
2002	1,165	659	35	471
2003	955	410	35	510
2004	557	212	11	334
2005	593	453	2	138
TOTAL	4656	2380	103	-

Source: Nigerian Code of Conduct Bureau
http://www.codeofconductbureau.com/establishmentCCB.html

The Constitution and the Code of Conduct Bureau and Tribunal Act Vol. 2 Cap C15 LFN 2004 also gives power to the Bureau to make declarations of assets of all public officers available for inspection by every Nigerian citizen on such terms and conditions as the National Assembly may prescribe. However no such conditions have been prescribed and citizens are yet to be allowed to inspect declarations of Assets in Nigeria.

5.4.0 Nigeria and the Regional Anti-Corruption War

Nigeria has wedged its regional anti-corruption war through manly two fronts; the ECOWAS Protocol on the Fight against Corruption; and the AU Convention on Preventing and Combating Corruption.

5.4.1 ECOWAS Protocol on the Fight against Corruption

The Economic Community of West Africa (ECOWAS) Protocol on the Fight against Corruption was signed on December 21, 2001. The Protocol has a total of 27 articles. Article 2 outlines the aims and objectives of the Protocol, which include the promotion and development of effective mechanisms by State Parties to prevent, suppress and eradicate corruption. Accordingly, Articles 3 and 4 deal with scope and jurisdiction respectively while article 5 lists preventive measures which States Parties are expected to take, including national laws, ethical guidelines and codes of conduct. Other preventive measures include procurement laws, whistleblower protection, participation of CSOs and NGOs, revenue laws, declaration of assets by public officials, domestic anticorruption agencies (ACAs) and press freedom.

Article 6 of the Protocol outlines what constitutes acts of corruption including the demand, or offering of pecuniary gifts by public officials directly or indirectly, in exchange for certain acts or omission or promises therefore conferring undue advantage. Acts of corruption as defined under the Protocol also include diversion of public goods, unaccounted wealth, over invoicing, bribery and other forms of illicit enrichment. Article 7 provides for the laundering of proceeds of corruption and similar criminal offences. Article 8 provides for the protection of witnesses, while Article 9 contains provision for assistance and protection of victims.

Article 10 provides for sanctions and measures to be applied by State Parties for infractions of the Protocol, while Article 11 provides for liability of legal persons, including criminal, civil or administrative liabilities. Liabilities may involve monetary sanctions, disqualification from commercial activities, judicial winding-up orders, and placements under judicial supervision. Article 12 deals with acts of corruption concerning foreign public officials, while Article 13 contains provisions for seizures and forfeiture of the proceeds of crime. Article 14 makes offenders under the Protocol subject to extradition. Article 15 provides for mutual legal assistance and law enforcement cooperation between the State Parties relating to the investigation and prosecution of acts of corruption. Article 16 obliges the State Parties to designate a Central Authority for the purpose of mutual legal assistance and cooperation.

Article 17 provides for application of time in respect of offences committed before the Protocol came into force, while Article 18 urges State Parties to work towards harmonizing their national laws for the purpose of realizing the objectives of the Protocol. Article 19 provides for the establishment of a technical commission to be known as the Anti-corruption Commission, with specific objectives. Article 20 provides for the relationship of the Protocol with other treaties. Article 22 provides for ratification and entry into force of the Protocol, upon ratification by at least nine (9) signatory States. Article 23 provides for the depository authority and registration of the Protocol instrument with the ECOWAS Executive Secretariate. Article 24 provides for accession to the Protocol by non-ECOWAS member states. Article 25 contains provision for amendments and revision of the Protocol by the State Parties. Article 26 provides for denunciation of the Protocol by State Parties, while Article 27 contains provisions for settlement of disputes between State Parties to the Protocol by the ECOWAS Court of Justice.

Table 5.8 Aid Dependency of ECOWAS Member States 2004

	Country	Net Development Assistance 2004 ($m)	% of Gross National Income
1.	Benin	343	9.3%
2.	Burkina Faso	553	12.6%
3.	Cote d'Ivoire	138	1.0%
4.	Gambia	58	15.7%
5.	Ghana	1,234	15.7%
6.	Guinea	256	7.4%
7.	Guinea-Bissau	69	28.2%
8.	Liberia	197	42.8%
9.	Mali	519	11.6%
10.	Niger	485	17.8%
11.	Nigeria	525	0.8%
12.	Senegal	953	13.5%

13.	Sierra Leone	326	33.2%
14.	Togo	55	3.0%

Source: Boom (2009)

In spite of being signed since 21 December 2001, the ECOWAS Protocol on the Fight against Corruption is yet to come into force. The Protocol will come into force upon its ratification by at least 9 signatory states. Anti-corruption laws and institutions across much of West Africa are widely criticized as being ineffective for a number of reasons. First is that the flow of revenues from oil and diamonds continue to be the object of extensive grand corruption. Secondly, West African countries are highly dependent on foreign aid (Table 5.8). This is especially the case for rebuilding war-torn countries like Liberia and Sierra Leone, as well as for the land-locked Sahel countries. Hence, they put up a show of compliance with "good governance" requirements in order to ensure the continuous flow of aid. Last but not the least; Governments endeavor not to alienate political allies at home through anti-corruption crackdowns (Alabi: 2003).

5.4.2 African Union Convention on Preventing and Combating Corruption

The AU Convention on Preventing and Combating Corruption was adopted by Heads of State and Governments of the Africa Union at their Summit in Maputo, Mozambique, on 12 July 2003 and entered into force on 5 August 2006.

The preamble to the 28-article Convention among others, expresses concern about the negative effect of corruption on the political, economic, social and cultural development of Africa, and recognizes the need to address the root causes of corruption through partnership between governments and all segments of the society.

Article 1 of the Convention deals with definition of terms, while article 2 states the objectives of the Convention which include to:

> Promote and strengthen the development in Africa by each State Party of mechanisms required to prevent, detect, punish and eradicate corruption and related offences in the public and private sectors.

Article 3 deals with the principles of the Convention which include transparency and accountability in the management of public affairs, and condemnation of acts of corruption.

Article 4 defines the scope of application of the Convention. It covers solicitation or acceptance, offering or granting, acts or omission, and diversion, in connection with corruption, illicit enrichment, as well as acts of collusion between State Parties. Article 5 sets out legislative and other measures to be adopted by State Parties including independent anticorruption agencies, public sector reforms, protection of informants and witnesses, and school education programmes. Article 6 covers laundering of the proceeds of corruption. It enjoins State Parties to take steps to criminalize the conversion, transfer or disposal of illicit property within its territory.

The fight against corruption and related offences in the public service is detailed in Article 7, and includes provisions for declaration of assets and code of conduct. It also provides that the immunity granted to some public officials shall not be an obstacle to the investigation and prosecution of suspects, subject however to national legislations. Article 8 provides for the offence of illicit enrichment, while article 9 guarantees access to information. Article 10 provides for transparency in the funding of political parties, article 11 extends the fight against corruption to the private sector, while article 12 incorporates the civil society and media as well.

Article 13 deals with jurisdiction, article 14 provides minimum guarantees of a fair trial, and article 16 deals with confiscation and seizure of the proceeds and instrumentalities of corruption, including the repatriation of proceeds of corruption. Article 17 provides for bank secrecy, enjoining State Parties not to invoke bank secrecy to deny any requests made pursuant to the provisions of the Convention. Article 18 provides for cooperation and mutual legal assistance among State Parties to prevent, detect, investigate and punish acts of corruption, while article 19 provides for wider international cooperation in the fight against corruption.

Article 20 provides for national authorities to act as liaisons for the purpose of effecting the provisions of the Convention. Article 21 provides for supremacy of the Convention in relationship with other agreements dealing with corruption. Articles 23, 24, 25, 26, 27, and 28 contain the final provisions of the Convention. They include such formalities as signatures, reservations, amendment, denunciation etc.

As of 2005, the Convention had been signed and ratified by Algeria, Burkina Faso, Burundi, Comoros, Congo, Libya, Lesotho, Madagascar, Mali, Namibia, Niger, Rwanda, South Africa, Tanzania and Uganda. Nigeria was among 25 countries that had signed the Convention but were yet to ratify it, while 13 other countries had neither signed nor ratified the Convention.

Nigeria signed the Convention on December 16, 2003 and ratified it on 26 November 2006, after it had already come into force. However, Nigeria is yet to domestic the provisions of the AU Convention as provided in Section 12 of the 1999 Constitution. Section 12(1) of the 1999 Constitution provides inter alia;

> No treaty between the Federation and any other country shall the force of law except to the extent to which any such treaty has been enacted by the National Assembly.

5.4.3 African Peer Review Mechanism (APRM) Report on Nigeria

Nigeria was among the first countries to accede to the APRM at the 6th meeting of the NEPAD Heads of State and Government Implementation Committee held in Abuja, on 9 March 2003. The APR Panel's Country Support Mission (CSM) was fielded to Nigeria from 21-24 March 2005. A stalemate necessitated the fielding of a follow-up mission in October 2006 (Jinadu: 2008). In undertaking the national self-assessment process, the APRM Master Questionnaire was domesticated and four research instruments – Desk Research, Mass Household Survey, Elite/

Decision Maker and Focus Group Discussions, were used. The draft Country Self-Assessment Report (CSAR) and National Programme of Action (NPOA) were collated by the end of 2006.

Following national elections held in Nigeria in April 2007, the new administration of President Umaru Yar'Adua ushered in changes in the management and administrative structure of the APRM at national level. Nigeria submitted its final CSAR and draft NPOA to the APR Panel in January 2008.

The APRM Country review Report on Nigeria summarized the main challenge facing the country as "…the paradox of poverty in the midst of plenty." The Report questioned why the greatest oil producer in sub-Saharan Africa has the world's third largest concentration of poor people. It also pointed out the challenge of reversing value and attitudinal practices acquired during its military history including issues such as promoting transparency and accountability, and most importantly, stemming corruption and the attendant practices of graft, bribery and nepotism.

On the theme of Democracy and Good Political Governance, the Report notes that the use of money in politics corrupts the electoral process, undermines the principle of good governance, and poses a great hindrance to the development of constitutional democracy in Nigeria. The Report also noted that anti-corruption institutions in the country were under-funded and are sometimes perceived to under the influence of the Chief Executive.

Coming to the theme of Economic Governance and Management, the Report notes that corruption and fraudulent practices are rampant in Nigeria, and remain a cause for concern for most stakeholders. It noted that corruption in the public sector and incidence of money laundering are believed to be very high. It acknowledged various legislative reforms and initiatives introduced by the Federal Government since 1999 to tackle these economic ills, but observed significant capacity constraints on the part of the anti-corruption agencies, as well as failure to take the anti-corruption war to state and local government levels.

On the theme of Corporate Governance, the Report notes the negative consequences of economic and financial crimes such as Advance Fee Fraud (419) on Nigeria, including decreased foreign direct investment. It observes that even though there are comprehensive laws for fighting these crimes, such as ICPC Act, Anti-Money Laundering Act, the Advance Fe Fraud Decree and EFFCC Act, these laws remained mostly ineffectual. It there called for necessary safeguards, including a whistleblower protection safeguard to be put in place, and advocated a active media role in terms of investigative and feature reporting.

Finally on the theme of Socio-Economic Development, the Report has it that lack of strong political will, lack of monitoring and evaluation mechanisms, weak political, civic and administrative leadership, endemic corruption at all levels of government and within the society at large, and the lack of an entrenched participatory approach to development all contribute to explaining Nigeria's paradox of poverty in the midst of plenty (APRM: 2008).

In conclusion, the APRM Country Review for Nigeria identified the scourge of corruption to be among the issues deserving further treatment having been identified in more than one thematic area of governance. According to the Report, the challenge of political and economic corruption primarily explains poverty in Nigeria, holding back economic growth and development and frustrating incentives to align budgetary allocations with development priorities.

5.5.0 Nigeria and the Global Anti-Corruption Framework

Nigeria has also participated in the global war against corruption as encapsulated in the United Nations Convention against Corruption (UNCAC).

5.5.1 United Nations Convention against Corruption (UNCAC)

The United Nations Convention against Corruption was adopted by the General Assembly of the United Nations on 31 October 2003 at its Headquarters in New York. The Convention entered into force on 14 December 2005, with 140 signatories and 95 ratifications/accessions as at 20 August 2007. This is in accordance with article 68 (1) which provides that;

> This Convention shall enter into force on the ninetieth day after the date of deposit of the thirtieth instrument of ratification, acceptance, approval or accession.

The Preamble to the Convention notes, among others, the threat that corruption poses to economic development, political stability and the due process of law. It also acknowledges the transnational nature of corruption, hence the need for international cooperation in combating it. It further recalls previous multilateral treaties in the field, including the Africa Union Convention on Preventing and Combating Corruption 2003.

The main body of the Convention is divided into eight chapters and 71 articles. Chapter one contains the general provisions of the Convention. Article 1 (a) of Chapter 1 outlines the purpose of the Convention which is, among others;

> To promote and strengthen measures to prevent and combat corruption more efficiently and effectively.

Chapter two deals with preventive measures, which include the establishment of national anti-corruption bodies and public sector reforms such as code of conduct for public officials and public procurement reforms. Provisions are also made for preventive measures in the private sector as well as participation of the society and measures to prevent money laundering.

Chapter three deals with criminalization and law enforcement, and takes steps to criminalize such actions as bribery of national and intergovernmental public officials, embezzlement, misappropriation, and illicit enrichment. Such actions also extend to the private sector. The chapter also provides for freezing, seizure and confiscation of proceeds of corruption and deals with the issues of jurisdiction as well as international cooperation in criminal prosecution.

Chapter four provides specifically for international cooperation, including the areas of extradition, mutual legal assistance and law enforcement cooperation. Chapter five dwells on assets recovery. Chapter six deals with technical assistance and information exchange. Chapter outlines mechanisms for implementation of the Convention, while chapter eight contains final provisions on such issues as implementation and entry into force of the Convention.

The United Nations Convention against Corruption is commended as setting a high international standard for the fight against corruption, as well as providing a framework for national governments to fight corruption and promote good governance at the domestic, regional and global levels.

Table 5.9 Major Powers Ratification of UNCAC

European Union	12 November 2008 AA
France	11 July 2005
Germany	–
Italy	5 October 2009
Japan	–
United Kingdom	9 February 2006
United States	30 October 2006

Source: UNODC

The Convention has been signed by at least 129 Member States, and ratified by the following: Algeria, Belarus, Benin, Brazil, Croatia, Djibouti, Ecuador, Egypt, El Salvador, France, Honduras, Hungary, Jordan, Kenya, Libya, Madagascar, Mauritius, Mexico, Namibia, Nigeria, Paraguay, Peru, Romania, Sierra Leone, South Africa, Sri Lanka, Togo, Turkmenistan, Uganda, and the United Republic of Tanzania.

Nigeria signed the UNCAC in December 2003 and ratified it in December 2004, but is yet to domesticate its provisions as provided under Section 12 (1) of the 1999 Constitution. Apart from France which ratified UNCAC in July 2005, EU, Italy, UK and US only ratified the Convention after December 2005 when it was already in force (Table 5.9). The provisions of UNCAC being a global document cannot be effectively enforced without the cooperation of the major powers.

Jude Uddoh, Ph.D.

Reference
Chapter Five

Abegunrin, Olayiwola (2006) "Nigerian Foreign Policy under the Obasanjo Administration" in Abegunrin, Olayiwola and Akomolafe, Olusoji (Eds) (2006) *Nigeria in Global Politics* New York, Nova Science Publishers, Inc. pp. 265 – 276

Adeniji, Olu (2005) "Costs and Dividends of Foreign Policy" in The Presidential Advisory Council on International Relations (2005) *Foreign Policy in Nigeria's Democratic Transition* Abuja. PAC, pp. 21 – 50.

Adenirokun, Kunle (2004) *Due Process Saves Nigeria N102 bn, Says Obasanjo* in THISDAY July 13, 2004. Page 1

Alabi, Niyi (2003) *Global Corruption Report 2003*. Berlin, Transparency International.

Anyaoku, Emeka (2005) "Preface" in PAC (2005) *Foreign Policy in Nigeria's Democratic Transition* Abuja, Presidential Advisory Committee on International Relations Pp. 5 – 12.

APRM (2008) *Federal Republic of Nigeria. Country Review Report No. 8.* South Africa, African Peer Review Mechanism www.nepad.org/www.aprm-international.org

Boom, Dirk (2009) *ECOWAS: How Regional Integration Works in West Africa* Federal Ministry for Economic Cooperation and Development. Germany

DMO (2005) *Nigeria's Debt Relief Deal with the Paris Club.* Debt Management Office. Abuja. Nigeria www.dmo.gov.ng

Ezea, Kenneth (2000) *Nigeria's New Foreign Policy Awakening* THISDAY, July 16, 2000 p.10

Hart Group (2006) *Nigerian Extractive Industry Transparency Initiative. Final Report.* December 2006 http://www.neiti.org.ng/files-pdf/ExecutiveSummary-31Dec06.pdf

HRW (2011) *Corruption on Trial? The Record of Nigeria's Economic and Financial Crimes Commission.* Human Rights Watch. New York

ICPC (2005) *Progress Report Sept 2000 – July 2005I* Independent Corrupt Practices and other Related Offences Commission www.icpcnigeria.com

Iliffe, John (2011) *Obasanjo, Nigeria and the World* Suffolk, James Currey

Jinadu, Adele L. (2008) *The African Peer Review Process in Nigeria.* Open Society Initiative for West Africa. Dakar-Fann. Senegal www.osiwa.org

NPC (2004) *National Economic Empowerment and Economic Development Strategy: Meeting Everyones' Needs* Abuja, National Planning Commission

Nweke Jr., Frank (2005) *A New National Image.* Interview by World Report International Ltd. London. info@worldreport-ind.com

Obasanjo, Olusegun (2005) "Keynote Address" in The Presidential Advisory Council on International Relations (2005) *Foreign Policy in Nigeria's Democratic Transition* Abuja. PAC, Pp. 13 – 19.

Ploch, Lauren (2008) *Nigeria: Current Issues.* CRS Report for Congress. Congressional Research Service. Order Code RL 33964

Reiffel, Lex (2005) *Resolving Nigeria's Paris Club Debt Problem: A Case of Non-Performing Creditors* The Brookings Institute, August 1, 2005 (Final Draft).

Saliu, H. A. (2005) "Perspectives on Shuttle Diplomacy" in in Saliu, Hassan A. (Ed) (2005) *Nigeria under Democratic Rule (1999 – 2003) Vol. 2* Ibadan, University Press Plc. Pp. 255 – 274

Saliu, H. A. and Omotola, J. S. (2005) "Nigerian Foreign Policy under Obasanjo" in Saliu, Hassan A. (Ed) (2005) *Nigeria under Democratic Rule (1999 – 2003) Vol. 2* Ibadan, University Press Plc. pp. 241 – 254

Shonekan, E. A. O. (1997) *Vision 2010 Committee Report* Abuja, The Presidency

Theobold, Robin (2000) "Conclusion: Prospect for Reform in a Globalized Economy" in Doig, Alan and Theobold, Robinson Eds (2000) *Corruption and Democratization,* Frank Cass, pp 149 – 159.

TWB/FMF (2006) *Utilization of Repatriated Abacha Loot: Results of the Field Monitoring Exercise.* Report Prepared by the World Bank with Cooperation from the Federal Ministry of Finance. Abuja.

Ugolor David, Nwafor Apollos, and Nardine John (2006) *Shadow Report of the PENFAR Monitoring Exercise"* Edo State, Nigerian Network on Stolen Assets.

United Nations (1999) *Speech by President Olusegun Obasanjo"* UN General Assembly. 54th Session. 10th Plenary Meeting. 23 Sept. 1999. NY. Pp. 8 – 12.

UNODC (2008) *Annual Report 2008* United Nations Office on Drugs and Crime. Vienna

Chapter Six

CONCLUSION

If a country is strong at home, it will be respected abroad. If it is weak at home, nobody will pay attention to what that country is doing abroad. In order to build a vibrant foreign policy, we must anchor it on a strong domestic policy (Osuntokun: 2009).

Introduction

In this concluding Chapter, we will summarize the findings of this research in line with the research statements, and proffer some suggestions.

6.1.0 Summary of Findings

The summary of our research findings are presented in line with our research statements as follows:

6.1.1 First Research Statement:

The conduct of a country's foreign policy is to complement domestic imperatives of maximizing the welfare and security of citizens.

It is clear from both perspectives of the historical antecedents of Nigerian foreign policy discussed in Chapter Three as well as Nigerian foreign policy under the Obasanjo administration (Chapter Four), that the country's foreign policy has always been predicated on the national interest, which in reducible in its barest form to the security and welfare of Nigerian citizens.

Nigeria's first Prime Minister – Alhaji (Sir) Abubakar Tafawa Balewa laid out the broad principles of Nigeria's foreign policy as including first and foremost; "Promotion of the national interest of the federation and of its citizens" (Olusanya and Akindele: 1986). What constitutes Nigeria's 'national interest' was officially defined in the Second National Development Plan, 1970-74, as:

- A united, strong and self-reliant nation;
- A great and dynamic economy;
- A just and egalitarian society;
- A land of bright and full opportunities for all citizens; and
- A free and democratic society

National interest is the common thread that runs through both domestic and foreign policy, and is reducible in its barest form to the security and welfare of Nigerian citizens (Eze: 2006).

Major Nzeogwu, General Ironsi, and Lt. Col (later General) Gowon each affirmed adherence to the foreign policy objectives and commitments of the First Republic. However, only General Gowon stayed in office long enough to make any meaningful impact on Nigeria's foreign policy in the face of the domestic political instability and national uncertainty at the time. The main foreign policy thrust and exertions of Gowon's regime were therefore dictated by domestic constraints of prosecuting the Nigerian civil war (1967 – 1970), and keeping the country as one indivisible entity (Adeniran: 1985).

The primacy of the national interest – the security and welfare of Nigerian citizens in the conduct of Nigerian foreign policy, has been retained by all subsequent administrations in the country. The Muhammed/Obasanjo regime (1975 – 1979) outlined their regimes' foreign policy as including; "The defence of Nigeria's sovereignty, independence and territorial integrity" (Adeniran: 1985). The Buhari/Idiagbon foreign policy was anchored on what came to be known as 'economic nationalism,' or revamping the domestic economy which was devastated by the profligacy of the Second Republic.

General Babangida adopted economic diplomacy as the main thrust of his regime's foreign policy, defined by his erstwhile Minister of Foreign Affairs – General Ike Nwachukwu, as the task of using foreign policy "to achieve Nigeria's economic development and economic goals" (Akinsanya et al: 1991).

Section 19 (a) of the Constitution of the Federal Republic of Nigeria operated by the Obasanjo administration, outliners objectives of Nigeria's foreign policy as primarily, the "promotion and protection of the national interest." The philosophical foundation of Obasanjo's foreign policy was variously expounded by his foreign affairs ministers – Alhaji Sule Lamido as the "foreign policy for democracy" project, underlined by the logic that democracy must provide concrete dividends for the people within the shortest possible time, and by Olu Adeniji, as a "beneficial concentricism" approach which aims to make Nigerians the primary beneficiary of the country's foreign policy by weaving economic gains into the expenditures and thrusts of Nigeria's foreign policy (Ezea: 2000, Adeniji: 2005).

Hence the pursuit of economic diplomacy by the Obasanjo administration is hinged on three pedestals; recovery of Nigeria's looted funds stashed abroad, campaign for debt forgiveness, and attraction of foreign direct investment (FDI) into the country (Saliu and Omotola: 2005).

Therefore, to the extent that successive civilian and military administrations in Nigeria have at least in principle anchored their foreign policy consistently on the national interest – the security and welfare of Nigerian citizens, we can affirm that our first research statement is true.

6.1.2 Second Research Statement:

Nigeria's endemic culture of corruption has undermined domestic desires for achieving the purpose of the state and particularly, has negatively impacted on the country's international image and foreign policy.

As stated earlier, national interest is the single thread that runs through both domestic and foreign policies. Therefore, the underpinning objective of Nigerian foreign policy is the domestic desire to achieve the purpose of the state which basically consists of the security and welfare of Nigerian citizens (see the First Research Statement above).

However, the preponderance of evidence from aspects of the literature review in Chapter Two; our study of the historical antecedents of corruption and Nigerian foreign (Chapter Three); as well as corruption and foreign policy under the administration of President Obasanjo (Chapter Four) indicate a recurrent pattern of endemic corruption which runs contrary to the purpose of the state.

In the First Republic of Alhaji (Sir) Abubakar Tafawa Balewa (1960 to 1966), Nnamdi Azikiwe was indicted of abusing his office by allowing public funds to be invested in the African Continental Bank (ACB) in which he had interests. Chief Obafemi Awolowo was also found guilty of diverting N4.4 million in cash and N1.3 million in overdraft from the Western Region Government-owned National Investment and Property Company, to finance the Action Group (AG) party and to build a personal financial empire (Osaghae: 1998).

The regime of General Yakubu Gowon administration (1966 to 1975) is remembered for the cement importation scandal, in which the cost of purchase and freight of 2.9 metric tons of cement was inflated by nearly 100% from $40 to $75 per ton. Nine out of eleven former military governors under the Gowon regime were found guilty of corruption involving embezzlement of public funds and gross abuse of office, and were made to forfeit assets worth over ten million naira to the State (Chuku: 2004).

A whooping N2.8 billion went missing from the account of the Nigerian National Petroleum Corporation (NNPC) during the regime of General Olusegun Obasanjo (1976 to 1979). The money was eventually traced to the London branch of Bank of Credit and Commerce International (BCCI) in which Alhaji Dasuki and General Shehu Musa Yaradua had substantial interests. However, interests accumulated on the money between 1977 and 1980 were never credited to Nigeria.

The Second Republic administration of Alhaji Shehu Shagari is notorious for its profligacy especially among the state governors and federal law makers. Within the first four years of the Second Republic administration of Alhaji Shehu Shagari (1979 to 1984), Nigeria earned about N40.5 billion in oil revenue and squandered it. Various Tribunals set up to probe the Shagari administration recovered over N112 million and £688,000 from politicians, over N348 million from FEDECO, and about N48.5 million from the National Assembly, within a year. N3.4 million was found "stacked up" in the home of Governor Bakin Zuwo of Kano State alone. However, attempts to recover looted monies stashed by politicians overseas as exemplified in the aborted kidnap attempt on Umaru Dikko, were unsuccessful (Osaghae: 1998).

Different accounts attribute the legitimization of corruption in Nigeria in what came to be known as the politics of settlement to the regime of General Ibrahim Babangida (1985 to 1993). The Babangida regime is particularly remembered for frittering away $12.4 billion Gulf War oil windfall accruing to Nigeria through the so-called "dedicated and special" accounts, in extra-budgetary expenditures over a period of about six years (Oko-Osi: 2007).

Transparency International estimates that General Sani Abacha (1993 to 1998) and his associates stole between $2 billion to $5 billion from the Nigerian treasury and placed him among the top five political looters of all time. General Abacha's shady deals include $2 billion Ajaokuta Steelworks debt buy-back and $190 million which ELF Aquitane admitted paying to him. The succeeding regime of General Abdulsalaami Abubakar recovered $500 million in cash from Ismail Gwarzo – Abacha's erstwhile National Security Adviser. By May 2009, some $1.9 billion had been recovered from the late Abacha family, and the whereabouts of another $700 million was also established (Iliffe: 2011).

Some cases of grand corruption during the Third Republic administration of President Olusegun Obasanjo (1999 to 2007) include conviction of Inspector General of Police Tafa Balogun of an 8-count charge of money laundering and sentencing to 6 months imprisonment as well as forfeiture of assets totaling $150 million; conviction of Governor Diepreye Alamieyesegha of Bayelsa State on a 6-count charge of false declaration of assets and a 23-count charge of money laundering by his companies leading to recovery of over $17.7 million in stolen assets; conviction of Chief Olabode George – Deputy National Chairman of PDP and Chairman of Nigerian Ports Authority and five others on a 35-count charge of contract inflation by N100 billion among others; and conviction of Delta State Governor James Ibori by a London court on a 10-count of conspiracy to defraud and money laundering estimated at $250 million.

In what was described as the single biggest case of advance fee fraud (AFF) in the whole world, four Nigerian nationals – Christian Anajemba, Emmanuel Nwude, Nzeribe Okoli and Amaka Anajemba defrauded Banco Noroeste S.A. of Brazil of a total of $242 million between May 1995 and February 1998, on the pretext of securing contracts for the construction of a second international airport in Abuja. President Obasanjo was to bequeath his successor Umar Musa Yaradua, with an election that was reported by both domestic and international observers as fraught with procedural irregularities, electoral fraud and voter disenfranchisement.

Corruption has been blamed for the series of military coups and political instability in Nigeria, as well as the country's economic backwardness and poverty on a massive scale "in the midst of plenty." The impact of corruption is not lost on Nigeria's foreign policy, as according to Nuamah (2003: 4);

> Corruption in Nigeria constrains the country's economic development and consequently its economic and political reach regionally and internationally (Nuamah: 2003: 4).

The impact of corruption on Nigeria's foreign policy is discussed in Chapter Four, includes loss of image; international isolation; lack of foreign direct investment/divestment; depletion of external reserves/ accumulation of foreign debts; and harassment of Nigerians abroad. Cumulatively, corruption robbed Nigeria of a strong and virile foreign policy. Corruption weakened the thrust and effectiveness of Nigerian foreign policy, and undermined the influence and respectability that out to have accrued to the country's foreign policy undertakings since independence (Izah: 1991, Abegunrin: 2003, Jega: 2010).

Therefore, our second research statement holds true to the extent that endemic corruption in Nigeria has both undermined the purpose of the state as well as impacting negatively on the country's international image and foreign policy.

6.1.3 Third Research Statement:

> Responding to Nigeria's corruption at home and abroad has played a critical role in shaping Nigeria's foreign policy under the Obasanjo administration.

The conditions of the domestic and external environments play major roles in determining a country's foreign policy, and both environments are related in a complex and intricate manner (Saliu: 1999).

The foreign policy of General Yakubu Gowon (1966 – 1975) was dictated by domestic constraints of prosecuting the Nigerian Civil War (1967 – 1970) and keeping the country as one indivisible political entity (Adeniran: 1985). Even after the war, the direction of Nigeria's foreign policy continued to be influence by the country's experience during the war and later by the soaring price of oil (Fawole: 2003).

Similarly, General Sani Abacha (1993 – 1998) did not articulate a clear foreign policy. Rather, his tragic domestic policies including his crackdown on pro-democracy activists, gross abuse of human rights and fundamental freedoms, the arrest and detention of Chief Abiola in June 1994, the March 1995 phantom coup, the November 1995 hanging of Ken Saro-Wiwa and eight Ogoni activists, and the controversial coup plot of December 1997 snowballed into diplomatic controversies and became the defining parameters of his regime's foreign policy (Fawole: 1999).

The foreign policy of President Olusegun Obasanjo (1999 – 2007) as we have seen in the preceding chapter was conditioned by the need to reverse the pariah status to which Nigeria was relegated as a result of several factors including the country's acquired image and reputation as a very corrupt country and nearly 16 years of autocratic military rule with attendant human rights abuse and disrespect for the rule of law. The impact of corruption on Nigeria's foreign policy as discussed in Chapter Four include loss of image, international isolation, lack of foreign direct investment/divestment, depletion of external reserves/ accumulation of foreign debt, and harassment of Nigerians abroad.

At the onset of the Obasanjo administration, Nigeria faced several sanctions imposed by the international community. Transparency International had ranked Nigeria as the most corrupt country in 1996 and 1997 consecutively, and again in 2000 (see Table 4.4). President Obasanjo noted during his inaugural speech that Nigeria, once a well-respected country and a key role player in international bodies, became a pariah nation;

> The impact of official corruption is so rampant and has earned Nigeria a very bad image at home and abroad. Besides, it has distorted and retrogressed development (Obasanjo: 1999).

He stated his administration's resolve to restore Nigeria fully to her previous prestigious position in the comity of nations, further pledging that; "All the impacts of bad governance on our people that are immediately removable will be removed, while working for medium and long term solutions."

Accordingly, President Olusegun Obasanjo set out to establish strong domestic anti-corruption institutions as well as collaboration with other countries at the regional and global levels in the anti-corruption realm with mixed results. The anti-corruption efforsts of the Obasanjo administration include the following:

- Establishment of two domestic anti-corruption agencies (ACAs); the Independent Corrupt Practices and other Related Offences Commission (ICPC) described as "the toughest anti-corruption law in the history of Nigeria;" and the Economic and Financial Crimes Commission (EFCC), charged with responsibility of enforcing various laws including the Advanced Fee Fraud and Other Related Offences Act 1995.
- Setting up of the Budget Monitoring and Price Intelligence Unit (BMPIU) otherwise known as "Due Process," with the objectives to among others, regulate government policies and practices on public procurement.

- Passing the Nigerian Extractive Industries Transparency Initiative (NEITI) Act 2007, with the primary responsibility of ensuring transparency and accountability in the extractive industry sector.
- Overhauling the operations of the Code of Conduct Bureau and vesting it with power to investigate public complaints of breaches of the constitutional provision of Code of Conduct for Public Officers.

At the regional levels, Nigeria under President Obasanjo, became a state-party to the ECOWAS Protocol on the Fight against Corruption which was signed on December 21, 2001 as a multilateral mechanism for fighting corruption. Nigeria also signed the AU Convention on Preventing and Combating Corruption on December 16, 2003 and ratified it on November 26, 2006. Article 2 of the AU Convention states the objectives of the Convention which include to:

> Promote and strengthen the development in Africa by each State Party of mechanisms required to prevent, detect, punish and eradicate corruption and related offences in the public and private sectors.

At the global level, the Obasanjo administration signed the UN Convention against Corruption (UNCAC) in December 2003 and ratified it a year later in December 2004. UNCAC aims among others;

> "To promote and strengthen measures to prevent and combat corruption more efficiently and effectively."

The United Nations Convention against Corruption is commended as setting a high international standard for the fight against corruption, as well as providing a framework for national governments to fight corruption and promote good governance at the domestic, regional and global levels.

Similarly, the four priorities of Obasanjo foreign policy – redeeming Nigeria's image, recovery of looted funds stashed abroad, campaigning for debt relief, and attracting foreign direct investment (FDI), all aimed at correcting damages that corruption had inflicted on the country. The last three items in the priority list also constitute what is described as the "economic diplomacy" of President Obasanjo's administration (Abegunrin: 2006, Saliu and Omotola: 2005).

The Obasanjo administration recorded some success in laundering Nigeria's image and reintegrating the country into the comity of nations. Through various strategies adopted by the administration including economic and anti-corruption reforms, shuttle diplomacy and official propaganda Nigeria's ranking in Transparency International's Corruption Perception Index (CPI) improved from being the most corrupt country in 2000 to the 9th position in 2007 (see Table 5.1). Former Secretary-General of the Commonwealth – Chief Emeka Anyaoku describes Nigeria's reintegration to the comity of nations under President Obasanjo in the following terms;

> Since 1999, Nigeria under our current President has reversed the international isolation to which we had been consigned as a result of our domestic situation which was characterized by major negations of the tenets of good governance. We are no longer a pariah state. We are now consulted on the major issues facing humanity, such as peace and stability in Africa, economic development, the environment and terrorism (Anyaoku: 2005:7).

In the area of recovery of looted funds stashed by General Sani Abacha and his associates abroad, President Obasanjo campaigned vigorously for the repatriation of Africa's looted funds stashed in foreign bank accounts at different fora, including the UN General Assembly (United Nations: 1999). Through concerted diplomatic and legal action, his administration secured the repatriation of over $500 million of the Abacha loot from Switzerland and other jurisdictions. However, some controversies trailed the utilization of the repatriated funds (see Table 5.2, FMF/TWB: 2006, Ugolor et al: 2006).

With regards to the campaign for debt relief, the Obasanjo administration was able to secure about 60% ($18 billion) cancellation

Corruption and Nigerian Foreign Policy (1999 - 2007)

out of the $36 billion Nigeria owed the Paris Club as of December 2004 (see Tables 4.6 and 5.3). The Obasanjo administration mounted a vigorous international campaign to achieve the Paris Club debt deal, even though Nigeria did not qualify for debt cancellation under the highly indebted poor countries (HIPC) guidelines. The Head of Good Governance Section of the European Commission delegation to Nigeria – Marc Friedrich, made the point, that;

> Although there were many factors that would have contributed to the Paris Club's decision but government's efforts at tackling corruption was one major factor the Club considered (Reiffel: 2005).

On the issue of foreign direct investment (FDI), the Obasanjo administration was able to turn around the tide of lack of FDI and divestment from Nigeria and achieve to achieve some measure of progress. For the most part of President Obasanjo's first term in office, FDI inflow into Nigeria was in a flux, fluctuating from $190.59 million in 1999 to $167.39 million in 2000 and from $13.96 million in 2001 to $271.22 million in 2002 due to several factors including poor governance and corruption, weak infrastructure and lack of security (UNCTAD: 2009).. Multinational corporations (MNCs) that divested from Nigeria during the Obasanjo administration include Michelin, Dunlop, Pfizer, Aventis, GlaxoWellcome and SmithKline Beecham (GlaxoSmithKline), Hoescht and Procter and Gamble (P&G). However, FDI inflow into Nigeria was consolidated in the later part of the Obasanjo administration with increases from $440.83 million in 2003 to $7,267.49 million in 2004 and further to $8,513.11 million in 2005 (see Table 5.4).

We can also answer the third research statement in the affirmative regarding the extent to which Nigeria's foreign policy under the Obasanjo administration was shaped by the need to respond to Nigeria's corruption at home and abroad (Quod erat demonstratum).

6.2.0 Suggestions

The suggestions deriving from our work are as follows:

As the saying goes, charity must begin at home. For too long, Nigeria has expended huge human, material and financial resources abroad in pursuing an idealistic foreign policy at the expense of the economic and social wellbeing of the domestic polity. Ukeje (1999) rightly counsels that "Nigeria should refrain from attempting to solve the continent's entire problem by itself." Nigeria itself should henceforth be the centerpiece of foreign policy. It is the responsibility of Government to address the issues of freedom from fear and want for both Nigerians at home and abroad, and provide citizens the necessary channels to realize their talents and ambition, thus tackling the underlying causes of corruption (Uzoigwe: 2004). Moreover, each of the concentric circles of Nigerian foreign policy should be imbued with tangible economic benefits for Nigerian citizens (Adeniji: 2005).

Nigeria's foreign policy think tank – the Nigerian Institute of International Affairs (NIIA) should focus additional research on how corruption affects Nigerian foreign policy and conversely, how Nigerian foreign policy could be used to fight corruption. The formal institutions of Nigerian foreign policy – the home ministry as well as foreign outposts, should be overhauled and made more responsive to the challenges that corruption poses for Nigerian foreign policy and its international image. Furthermore, Nigerian policing agents and diplomats overseas should participate more actively, in conjunction with their host countries, in preventive as well as enforcement anti-corruption measures (Mustapha: 2008). Government should appoint more of career diplomats than politicians to head Nigeria's foreign missions in order to enhance professionalism as well as greater transparency and accountability.

Nigeria should strengthen the domestic anti-corruption agencies (ACAs) in order to improve on their performance. In particular, the ICPC should be adequately funded in terms of both capital and recurrent expenditures in order to carry out its functions effectively. Part of the stolen funds repatriated from overseas should be channeled to funding the ACAs. Section 3 (2) of the EFCC (Establishment) Act which fetters the independence of the Commission from political and executive influence should be amended or repealed for the Commission to be truly independent. It is also suggested that special courts be set up to try corruption-related offences, with a view to avoiding the long delays inherent in the operation of the regular courts.

Nigeria should take steps in conjunction with other countries in the West African sub-region to garner sufficient ratifications necessary to bring the ECOWAS Protocol on the Fight against Corruption into force. The fact that the Protocol was signed since 2001 but is yet to come into force is an indication of lack of political will on the part of ECOWAS member states to seriously tackle corruption in the sub-region. Nigeria should also take steps to enact those anti-corruption conventions to which it is a state party as part of the body of its domestic laws as provided under Section 12 of the Constitution of the Federal Republic of Nigeria (CFRN) 1999. It is only when such anti-corruption treaties are domesticated that they can become operational in the country. According to the Socio-Economic rights and Accountability Project (SERAP);

> The domestication of the UN Convention against Corruption would stimulate increased respect for the principles of transparency and accountability in the governance of Nigeria; increase its impact domestically as well as strengthen its judicial enforcement.

Nigeria should strengthen its bilateral cooperation with the industrialized nations in the anti-corruption realm particularly in the areas of prosecution of offenders and recovery of stolen assets. Such cooperation in the past as in the cases of Governor D. S. P. Alamieyesegha of Bayelsa State, and Governor James Ibori of Delta, have been shown to yield positive results. Finally, Nigeria should align with other developing countries to pressurize the industrialized nations into fully ratifying UNCAC, as well as in doing more to prevent, detect and punish the involvement of their citizens and corporations in foreign corrupt practices.

References
Chapter Six

Abegunrin, Olayiwola (2003) *Nigerian Foreign Policy under Military Rule, 1966-1999* Westport, Praeger Publishers

Abegunrin, Olayiwola (2006) "Nigerian Foreign Policy under the Obasanjo Administration" in Abegunrin, Olayiwola and Akomolafe, Olusoji (Eds) (2006) *Nigeria in Global Politics* New York, Nova Science Publishers, Inc. pp. 265 – 276

Adebajo, Adekeye (2008) "Mad Dog and Glory: Nigeria's Intervention in Liberia and Sierra Leone" in Adebajo Adekeye and Mustapha Abdul Raufu (2008) *Gulliver's Trouble: Nigeria's Foreign Policy after the Cold War* South Africa, University of KwaZulu-Natal Press Pp. 177 – 202.

Adeniji, Olu (2005) "Costs and Dividends of Foreign Policy" in The Presidential Advisory Council on International Relations (2005) *Foreign Policy in Nigeria's Democratic Transition* Abuja. PAC, pp. 21 – 50.

Adeniji, Olu (2005) "Costs and Dividends of Foreign Policy" in The Presidential Advisory Council on International Relations (2005) *Foreign Policy in Nigeria's Democratic Transition* Abuja. PAC, pp 21 – 50.

Adeniran, Tunde (1985) "The Terrain and Tenor of Nigeria's Foreign Policy" in Atanda J. A. and Aliyu, A. Y. (Eds) (1985) *Proceedings of the National Conference on Nigeria since Independence. Volume : Political Development.* Zaria, The Panel on Nigeria Since Independence History Project. Pp. 188 – 201.

Agedah, Dickson (1993) *Corruption and the Stability of the Third Republic* Lagos, Perception Publications

Akinsanya, Olusegun et al (1991) *Nigeria's Economic Diplomacy (The Ike Nwachukwu Years, 1988 – 1992)* Nigeria, Ministry of Foreign Affairs

Akinterinwa, Bola A. (2007) *General Ibrahim Babangida's Legacy: Domestic and International Dimensions* Malthouse Monographs on Africa No. 5. Lagos, Malthouse Press Limited. Pp. 47 – 82.

Anyaoku, Emeka (2005) "Preface" in PAC (2005) *Foreign Policy in Nigeria's Democratic Transition* Abuja, Presidential Advisory Committee on International Relations Pp. 5 – 12.

APRM (2008) *Nigeria: Country Review Report No. 8* South Africa, African Peer Review Mechanism

Bray, J (1999) *Surveying Corruption,* London, Control Risks Group

Eze, Osita C. (2005) *Nigeria's Multilateral Diplomacy – UNO, WTO, World Bank, IMF, Commonwealth* in The Presidential Advisory Council on International Relations (2005) *Foreign Policy in Nigeria's Democratic Transition* Abuja. PAC, pp. 118 – 141.

Ezea, Kenneth (2000) *Nigeria's New Foreign Policy Awakening* THISDAY, July 16, 2000 p.10

Fafowora, Oladapo (1997) *Nigeria: Foreign Policy and Diplomatic Disarray* African Journal of International Affairs, Vol. 1, No. 1, 1997

Fawole, Alade W (2003) *Nigeria's External Relations and Foreign Policy under Military Rule, 1966 – 1999* Ile-Ife, Obafemi Awolowo University Press Ltd.

Fawole, Alade W. (1999) *Paranoia, Hostility and Defiance: General Sani Abacha and the "New" Nigerian Foreign Policy* Ile-Ife, Obafemi Awolowo University Press

Iliffe, John (2011) *Obasanjo, Nigeria and the World* Suffolk, James Currey

Izah, Paul P. (1991) *Continuity and Change in Nigerian foreign policy* Zaria, Ahmadu Bello University Press

Jude Uddoh, Ph.D.

Jega, Attahiru M. (2010) "Nigeria's Foreign Policy and the Promotion of Peace, Development, and Democracy," in Jega, Attahiru M. and Farris, Jacqueline W. (Eds.) (2010) *Nigeria at Fifty: Contributions to Peace, Democracy and Development* Abuja, The Shehu Musa Yar'Adua Foundation

Leatherwood, David G. (2001) *Peacekeeping in West Africa* Loint Force Quarterly, Autumn-Winter, 2001

Mustapha, Abdul Faufu (2008) "Challenges for Nigeria's Foreign Policy in the Post-Cold War Era," in Adebajo Adekeye and Mustapha Abdul Raufu (2008) *Gulliver's Trouble: Nigeria's Foreign Policy after the Cold War* South Africa, University of KwaZulu-Natal Press Pp. 369 - 382

Nuamah, Rosemary Rpt. (2003) *Nigeria's Foreign Policy after the Cold War: Domestic, Regional and External Influence* UK, Oxford University Press.

Ogwu, Joy (2005) *National Reputation and the Logic of Rebuilding Nigeria's Foreign Image* The Guardian October 20, 2005 Page 8

Osaghae, Eghosa E. (1998) *Crippled Giant: Nigeria since Independence* Bloomington, Indiana University Press

Osuntokun, Jide (2009) *We Must be Strong at Home for our Foreign Policy to be Meaningful Abroad* Interview granted to Adekoya Adekunle VANGUARD Thursday March 19, 2009

Reiffel, Lex (2005) *Resolving Nigeria's Paris Club Debt Problem: A Case of Non-Performing Creditors* The Brookings Institute, August 1, 2005 (Final Draft).

Saliu, H. A. and Omotola, J. S. (2005) "Nigerian Foreign Policy under Obasanjo" in Saliu, Hassan A. (Ed) (2005) *Nigeria under Democratic Rule (1999 – 2003) Vol. 2* Ibadan, University Press Plc. pp. 241 – 254

Saliu, Hassan A. (1999) "Limitations of Nigerian Foreign Policy" in Aliu, Hasan A (Ed) (1999) *Selected Themes in Nigerian Foreign Policy and International relations* Ilorin, Sally and Associates pp. 121 – 140

Shoneka, E. A. O. (1997) *Vision 2010 Committee Vol. 1 Main Report* Abuja, The Presidency

Ugolor David, Nwafor Apollos, and Nardine John (2006) *Shadow Report of the PENFAR Monitoring Exercise*" Edo State, Nigerian Network on Stolen Assets.

Ukeje, Inno (1999) *Nigerian Foreign Policy and Great Power Politics: Options for Nigerian Diplomacy in the 21st Century* Abuja, Chinedum Publishers

UNCTAD (2009) *Nigeria: Investment Policy review.* New York, United Nations Conference on Trade and Development

Uzoigwe, G. N. (2004) "The Future of Nigeria: Problems and Prospects in the Twenty-first Century" in Nwachuku, Levi A and Uzoigwe G. N. (2004) *Trouble Journey: Nigeria since the Civil War* Dallas, University Press of America.

Wei, S (1998) *How Taxing is Corruption on International Investors? USA,* Harvard University

BIBLIOGRAPHY

Textbooks

Abegunrin, Olayiwola (2003) *Nigerian Foreign Policy under Military Rule, 1966-1999* Westport, Praeger Publishers

Abegunrin, Olayiwola and Akomolafe, Olusoji (Eds) (2006) *Nigeria in Global Politics* New York, Nova Science Publishers, Inc.

Adebajo Adekeye and Mustapha Abdul Raufu (Eds) (2008) *Gulliver's Trouble: Nigeria's Foreign Policy after the Cold War* South Africa, University of KwaZulu-Natal Press

Adebanwi, Wale (2012) *Authority Stealing: Anti-Corruption War and Democratic Politics in Post-Military Nigeria* Durham, Carolina Academic Press

Adetula, Victor (Ed) (2008) *Money and Politics in Nigeria* Abuja, International Foundation for Electoral System

Agedah, Dickson (1993) *Corruption and the Stability of the Third Republic* Lagos, Perception Publications

Akinsanya, Olusegun et al (1991) *Nigeria's Economic Diplomacy (The Ike Nwachukwu Years, 1988 – 1992)* Nigeria, Ministry of Foreign Affairs

Aliu, Hasan A (Ed) (1999) *Selected Themes in Nigerian Foreign Policy and InternationalRrelations* Ilorin, Sally and Associates

Andvig J. C. and Fjeldstad O. (2000) *Research on Corruption: A Policy Oriented Survey* Oslo, Norwegian Institute of International Affairs

Boom, Dirk (2009) *ECOWAS: How Regional Integration Works in West Africa* Federal Ministry for Economic Cooperation and Development. Germany

Campbell, John (2011) *Nigeria: Dancing on the Brink* New York, Rowman & Littlefield Publishers, Inc

Diamond Larry, Kirk-Green Anthony, and Oyediran Oyeleye (Eds) (1997) *Transition Without End: Nigerian Politics and Civil Society under Babangida* London, Lynne Rienner Publishers

Doig, Alan and Theobold, Robinson Eds (2000) *Corruption and Democratization,* London, Frank Cass

Fawole, Alade W (2003) *Nigeria's External Relations and Foreign Policy under Military Rule, 1966 – 1999* Ile-Ife, Obafemi Awolowo University Press Ltd.

Fawole, Alade W. (1999) *Paranoia, Hostility and Defiance: General Sani Abacha and the "New" Nigerian Foreign Policy* Ile-Ife, Obafemi Awolowo University Press

Heidenheimer, Arnold J., Ed. (1970) *Political Corruption: Readings in Comparative Analysis* New Jersey, Transaction Books.

Ihonvbere, Julis O. and Shaw, Timothy (1998) *Illusions of Power: Nigeria in Transition* New Jersey, Africa World Press, Inc.

Iliffe, John (2011) *Obasanjo, Nigeria and the World* Suffolk, James Currey

Iroanusi, Sam O. (2006) *Corruption: The Nigerian Example* Lagos Sam Iroanusi Publications

Izah, Paul P. (1991) *Continuity and Change in Nigerian foreign policy* Zaria, Ahmadu Bello University Press

Jega, Attahiru M. and Farris, Jacqueline W. (Eds.) (2010) *Nigeria at Fifty: Contributions to Peace, Democracy and Development* Abuja, The Shehu Musa Yar'Adua Foundation

Mbaku, John M. (1998) *Corruption and the Crisis of Institutional Reforms in Africa* Lewiston, Edwin Mellen Press.

Mbaku, John M. (2000) *Bureaucratic and Political Corruption in Africa: the Public Choice Perspective* Florida, Krieger Publishing Company

Nuamah, Rosemary Rpt. (2003) *Nigeria's Foreign Policy after the Cold War: Domestic, Regional and External Influence* United Kingdom, Oxford University Press

Nwabueze, Ben (2007) *How President Obasanjo Subverted the Rule of Law and Democracy* Ibadan, Gold Press Limited

Nwachuku, Levi A. and Uzoigwe, G. N. (2004) *Trouble Journey: Nigeria Since the Civil War* Dallas, University Press of America Inc.

Ofo, Janet E. (1994) *Research Methods and Statistics in Education and Social Sciences* Lagos, Joja Publishers Ltd.

Olusanya G. O. and Akindele R. A. (Eds) (1986) *Nigeria's External Relations: The First Twenty Five Years* Ibadan, The University Press Limited

Olusanya, Gabriel O. and Akindele, R. A. (Eds) (1990) *The Structure and Processes of Foreign Policy Making and Implementation in Nigeria, 1960 – 1990* Lagos, NIIA

Osaghae, Eghosa E. (1998) *Crippled Giant: Nigeria since Independence* Bloomington, Indiana University Press

PAC (2005) *Foreign Policy in Nigeria's Democratic Transition* Abuja, The Presidential Advisory Council on International Relations

Rosenau, James N. (1969) *Linkage Politics* New York, The Free Press

Saliu, Hassan A. (Ed) (2005) *Nigeria under Democratic Rule (1999 – 2003) Vol. 2* Ibadan, University Press Plc.

Saliu, Hassan A. (Ed.) (1999) *Selected Themes in Nigerian Foreign Policy & International Relations* Ilorin, Sally and Associates

Ukeje, Inno (1999) *Nigerian Foreign Policy and Great Power Politics: Options for Nigerian Diplomacy in the 21ˢᵗ Century* Abuja, Chinedum Publishers

Wright, Stephen (1998) *Nigeria: Struggle for Stability and Status* Boulder, Westview Press

Journals and Specialized Publications

.Nwankwo, Adaora (2006) *The Determinants of Foreign Direct Investment Inflows (FDI) in Nigeria* 6ᵗʰ Global Conference on Business & Economics. Gutman Conference Center, USA

Abacha, Sani (1993) Coup Speech of November 17, 1993 http://www.citizensfornigeria.com/library/speeches/1211-coup-speech-of-general-sani-abacha-november-17-1993

Akinterinwa, Bola A. (2007) *General Ibrahim Babangida's Legacy: Domestic and International Dimensions* Malthouse Monographs on Africa No. 5. Lagos, Malthouse Press Limited. Pp. 47 – 82.

Alabi, Niyi (2003) *Global Corruption Report 2003*. Transparency International. Berlin www.transparency.org

APRM (2008) *Nigeria: Country Review Report No. 8*. South Africa, African Peer Review Mechanism www.nepad.org/www.aprm-international.org

Asobie, Asisi H. (1990) "Nigeria: Economic Diplomacy and National Interest. An Analysis of the Policies of Nigeria's External Economic Relations, with Special Reference to Ibrahim Babangida's Administration. Paper presented at the 16th Annual Conference of the Nigerian Society of International Affairs. Lagos, NIIA Nov. 5 – 6, 1990. P. 20

Atanda J. A. and Aliyu, A. Y. (Eds) (1985) *Proceedings of the National Conference on Nigeria since Independence. Volume 2: Political Development.* Zaria, the Panel on Nigeria Since Independence History Project.

Bray, J (1999) *Surveying Corruption,* London, Control Risks Group

Cookey, Samuel J. (1987) *Report of the Political Bureau* Lagos, Federal Government Printer

DMO (2005) *Nigeria's Debt Relief Deal with the Paris Club.* Debt Management Office. Abuja. Nigeria www.dmo.gov.ng

Edwards Angell Palmer & Dodge (2008) *Recovering Stolen Assets: A Case Study* IBA Conference Paris, 24 – 25 April, 2008

Eigen, Peter (2000) *Transparency International Releases the Year 2000 Corruption Perception Index* TI Newsletter www.transparency.org

Ekeanyanwu Lillian, Loremikan Shina, Ikubaje John (2004) *The National Integrity System, TI Country Study Report, Nigeria 2004* Berlin, Transparency International

EU EOM (2007) *Nigeria: Presidential, National Assembly, Gubernatorial, and State House of Assembly Elections. Final Report* Abuja, European Union Election Observation Mission.

Fafowora, Oladapo (1997) *Nigeria: Foreign Policy and Diplomatic Disarray* African Journal of International Affairs, Vol. 1, No. 1, 1997

Jude Uddoh, Ph.D.

Glynn Patrick, Kobrin Stephen J, Naim Moises (1997) *The Globalization of Corruption* Institute for International Economics http://www.iie.com

Hart Group (2006) *Nigerian Extractive Industry Transparency Initiative. Final Report.* December 2006   http://www.neiti.org.ng/files-pdf/ExecutiveSummaryFinal-31Dec06.pdf

HRW (2011) *Corruption on Trial? The Record of Nigeria's Economic and Financial Crimes Commission.* Human Rights Watch. New York http://www.neiti.org.ng/files-pdf/ExecutiveSummaryFinal-31Dec06.pdf

ICPC (2005) *Progress Report Sept 2000 – July 2005I* Independent Corrupt Practices and other Related Offences Commission www.icpcnigeria.com

IRI (2007) *Federal Republic of Nigeria State and National Elections April 14 and 21, 2007: Election Observation Final Report* Washington DC, The International Republican Institute

Isa, Lawal J. (Ed) (1995) *Not in Our Character: Proceeding of the National Seminar on the Appraisal of the Social and Moral Image of the Nigerian Society* Kaduna, Kaduna State Government

Jinadu, Adele L. (2008) *The African Peer Review Process in Nigeria.* Open Society Initiative for West Africa. Dakar-Fann. Senegal www.osiwa.org

Leatherwood, David G. (2001) *Peacekeeping in West Africa* Loint Force Quarterly, Autumn-Winter, 2001

Leiken, Robert S. (1996) *Controlling the Global Corruption Epidemic* Foreign Policy No. 105 (Winter, 1996-1997) Pp. 55 – 73.

Metz, Helen C. (Ed) (1991) *Nigeria: A Country Study.* Washington, Library of Congress

Ministry of Finance (2003) *The Nigerian Governance and Corruption Study.* University of Zaria, Zaria

NDI (2008) *Final NDI Report on Nigeria's 2007 Elections* Washington DC, National Democratic Institute

NPC (2004) *National Economic Empowerment and Economic Development Strategy: Meeting Everyones' Needs* Abuja, National Planning Commission

Nweke Jr., Frank (2005) *A New National Image.* Interview by World Report International Ltd. London. info@worldreport-ind.com

Nwosu, Nereus I (2007) *Nigeria's Foreign Policy under General Babangida* Malthouse Monographs on Africa. Nos. 6. Lagos, Malthouse Press Limited. Pp. 89 – 116.

Nzeogwu, Chukwuma K. (1966) *Radio Broadcast Announcing Nigeria's First Military Coup on Radio Nigeria, Kaduna* Vanguard September 30, 2010

Obasanjo, Olusegun 1999, *Inaugural Speech* West Africa Review: 1, 1. www.icaap.org/iuicode?101.1.1.1Obasanjo: 2005

Oko-Osi, Antonia T. (2007) *Corruption and Corrupt Practices: Institutionalization and Legitimization under the Babangida Administration* Malthouse Monographs on Africa No. 7. Lagos, Malthouse Press Limited pp. 8 – 33.

Peel, Michael (2006) *Nigeria-Related Financial Crime and Its Links with Britain.* Chattam House, London (UNODC: 2005).

Ploch, Lauren (2008) *Nigeria: Current Issues.* CRS Report for Congress. Congressional Research Services. The Library of Congress. Order Code RL 33964.

Reiffel, Lex (2005) *Resolving Nigeria's Paris Club Debt Problem: A Case of Non-Performing Creditors* The Brookings Institute, August 1, 2005 (Final Draft).

Ribadu, Nuhu (2006) *Nigeria's Struggle with Corruption* A Presentation to the US Congressional House Committee on International Development. Washington DC. May 18, 2006

Shoneka, E. A. O. (1997) *Vision 2010 Committee Vol. 1 Main Report* Abuja, The Presidency

Short, Claire (1999) *Combating Corruption, Promoting Development* London, Department for International Development (DFID)

Sowunmi A, Raufu A. A, Oketokun F. O, Salako M. A, and Usifoh O. O, (2010) *The Role of Media in Curbing Corruption in Nigeria* Research Journal of Information Technology 2(1): 7-23, May 20, 2010

The World Bank (1997) *World Development Report 1997: The State in a Changing World* New York, Oxford University Press

Transparency for Nigeria (2003)   http://transparencyng.com/index.php?option=com_content&view=article&id=449:-inspector-general-tafa-balogun-convicted-jailed-for-six-months&catid=86:law-crime-a-judiciary&Itemid=151

TWB/FMF (2006) *Utilization of Repatriated Abacha Loot: Results of the Field Monitoring Exercise.* Report Prepared by the World Bank with Cooperation from the Federal Ministry of Finance. Abuja.

Ugolor David, Nwafor Apollos, and Nardine John (2006) *Shadow Report of the PENFAR Monitoring Exercise"* Nigerian Network on Stolen Assets. Edo State. Nigeria

UNCTAD (2009) *Nigeria: Investment Policy review.* New York, United Nations Conference on Trade and Development www.nigeriamuse.com/nigeriawatch/officialfraud

United Nations (1999) *Speech by President Olusegun Obasanjo"* UN General Assembly. 54th Session. 10th Plenary Meeting. 23 Sept. 1999. New York. Pp. 8 – 12.

United Nations (2005) *Compendium of International Legal Instruments on Corruption 2ⁿᵈ Edition* New York, United Nations

UNODC (2005) *Transnational Organized Crime in the West African Region*. Vienna, United Nations Office on Drugs and Crime

UNODC (2008) *Annual Report 2008* United Nations Office on Drugs and Crime. Vienna

US Dept of State (1997) *Nigerian Advanced Fee Fraud* Washington, Bureau of International Narcotics and Law Enforcement Affairs

Van Vuuren, Hennie (2002) *Corruption, Perception and Foreign Direct Investment: Counting the Cost of Graft*. African Security Review Vol. 11 No. 3 2002

Wei, S (1998) *How Taxing is Corruption on International Investors? USA,* Harvard University

Newspapers and Periodicals

Abdulah, Abdulwahab (2009) *My Friends Deserted Me in Prison* Interview with Bode George Vanguard February 18, 2911.

Adebowale, Yemi (2007) *Adebayo, Olarenwaju, Others Named in 10m Euro Bribe* THISDAY Saturday November 17, 2007.

Adegoroye, Biyi (2011) *Nigeria's National Interest: Foreign Policy Focus* National Mirror June 29, 2012

Adenirokun, Kunle (2004) *Due Process Saves Nigeria N102 bn, Says Obasanjo* in THISDAY July 13, 2004. Page 1

Ajaero, Chris (2012) *Ibori's Long Road to Jail* Newswatch Magazine Sunday May 13, 2012 http://www.newswatchngr.com

Ezea, Kenneth (2000) *Nigeria's New Foreign Policy Awakening* THISDAY, July 16, 2000 p.10

Ogwu, Joy (2005) *National Reputation and the Logic of Rebuilding Nigeria's Foreign Image* The Guardian October 20, 2005 Page 8

Okiro, Mike (2009) *Report on the Halliburton Bribery Scandal in Nigeria* http://www.nigerianmuse.com/20100528080207zg/nigeria-watch/ official-fraud-watch-towards-fraud-free-governance-in-nigeria/text-of-report-on-the-halliburton-bribery-scandal-in-nigeria-by-a-panel-chaired-by-igp-mike/

Osuntokun, Jide (2009) *We Must be Strong at Home for our Foreign Policy to be Meaningful Abroad* Interview granted to Adekoya Adekunle VANGUARD Thursday March 19, 2009

ABOUT THE AUTHOR

Dr. Jude Uddoh earned his first degree in law and was called to the Nigerian bar in 1992. He also holds graduate qualifications in International Relations, including a doctorate degree from the University of Port Harcourt and a Certificate of Professional Achievement in Critical Issues in International Relations from Columbia University in the City of New York. Dr. Uddoh's research works cover African development, human rights, good governance, and security. Dr. Jude Uddoh has over fifteen years law practice experience in Nigeria. He has also worked as a consultant for Transparency International UK Defence and Security Programme (TI-DSP) and has served as a reader for President Barack Obama's Young African Leaders Initiative (YALI). Dr. Uddoh is currently an international affairs consultant. He lives in New York with his wife and three children.

www.ingramcontent.com/pod-product-compliance
Lightning Source LLC
Chambersburg PA
CBHW021542200526
45163CB00014B/741